British Columbia

A traveler's guide to the

HiSToRY

fascinating facts, intriguing

ALoNG The

incidents and lively legends

HiGHWaYs &

of Vancouver Island &

WaTeRWaYs

the British Columbia Coast

British Columbia

A traveler's guide to the

HiSToRY

fascinating facts, intriguing

ALoNG The

incidents and lively legends

HiGHWaYs &

of Vancouver Island &

WaTeRWaYs

the British Columbia Coast

Ted Stone

Red Deer College Press

The Publishers
Red Deer College Press
56 Avenue & 32 Street Box 5005
Red Deer Alberta Canada T4N 5H5

Acknowledgments
Edited for the Press by Bob Weber.
Cover design by Kunz + Associates.
Text design by Dennis Johnson.
Printed and bound in Canada by Webcom Limited for Red Deer College
Press.

Financial support provided by the Alberta Foundation for the Arts, a
beneficiary of the Lottery Fund of the Government of Alberta, and by
the Canada Council, the Department of Canadian Heritage and Red
Deer College.

COMMITTED TO THE DEVELOPMENT OF CULTURE AND THE ARTS

THE CANADA COUNCIL | LE CONSEIL DES ARTS
FOR THE ARTS | DU CANADA
SINCE 1957 | DEPUIS 1957

5 4 3 2 1

Canadian Cataloguing in Publication Data
Stone, Ted, 1947–
British Columbia history along the highways & waterways
(History along the highway)
Includes index.
ISBN 0-88995-173-X
1. Pacific Coast (B.C.)—History, Local. 2 Historic sites—Pacific Coast
(B.C.)—Guidebooks. 3. Automobile travel—Pacific Coast (B.C.)—
Guidebooks. 4. Pacific Coast (B.C.)—Guidebooks. 5. Vancouver Island
(B.C.)—Guidebooks. I. Title. II. Series.
FC3845.P2S76 1998   917.11'1044   C98-910248-3
F1087.S76 1998

For Patricia Pidlaski

Contents

Preface

THERE ARE MANY WAYS to explore the British Columbia coast. It might mean driving the twisty Island Highway along the eastern shore of Vancouver Island or following a logging road to an isolated beach. It might involve hiking the West Coast Trail, boating to a marine park, or sailing on a British Columbia or Alaska state ferry or even a luxury cruise ship up the Inside Passage. It could be just poking about the streets of downtown Nanaimo, Gibsons or any other coastal community. You might walk, drive, take a pleasure boat or paddle a canoe or kayak.

But traveling along the thousands of miles of British Columbia shoreline can be difficult. The coast here is gouged and slashed again and again by deep fjords and high mountains. On the west side of Vancouver Island and the north mainland coast, roads are almost entirely absent. It's simply too difficult and expensive to build them. Indeed, land along the British Columbia coast is so rugged and inhospitable that even walking it is a daunting prospect. Roaring tides can also make traveling by boat dangerous, although for most of the coast, waterways are the only practical way to get around. That reliance on waterways, though, is why this book is called *British Columbia History Along the Highways & Waterways.* Like a coastal traveler, the book eventually had to leave the highways behind to get where it wanted to go.

This is a book written for travelers on the coast, but it's not a town-by-town travel guide or a collection of local histories. And although the book focuses on the history of Vancouver Island and the rest of British Columbia's coast, it's not intended to be a full rendering of coastal history. It's goal is simpler. It is to provide an overview of the history of the province of British Columbia based on anecdotes and stories found along its coast. As I've retraced my travels on paper, I've assembled a sampling of the thousands of fascinating tales based on points of historical interest and that collectively offer an overview of coastal history.

No one can tell all the stories to be discovered up and down the coast from Victoria to Prince Rupert. A writer has to pick and choose tales from 200 years of recorded history on the coast and the much older accounts in aboriginal history as well. As someone who has lived and traveled on the coast, I've assembled here the stories that appealed to me, stories that made me laugh or feel sad, or that are just simply remarkable. It's my hope that *British Columbia History Along the Highways & Waterways* will stimulate you to look deeper into the history of the coast and to learn more stories about the people who settled this unique region of North America.

Introduction
History on the Coast

THE FOREST-COVERED ISLANDS, jagged inlets and windswept shores of the British Columbia coast combine to create some of the most powerfully beautiful landscapes in North America. The ragged coastal shoreline, just 650 miles (1,046 km) as the crow flies between Washington and Alaska, juts, jabs and folds back on itself for more than 20,000 miles (32,186 km)—a distance greater than the circumference of the world at the 49th parallel. Fjords cut dozens of miles into the heart of the mainland mountains, sometimes with rock-faced shores so steep that the land becomes inaccessible from the water. Arbutus trees with peeling red bark reach out like lonely sentinels on boulder-strewn southern beaches. Giant cedars and firs crowd above the shorelines of quiet island harbors. Snow-covered mountain peaks haunt the distance.

Humans first came to this stunning geography thousands of years ago, when the retreating glaciers allowed them in. Twenty thousand years ago, glaciers covered all of British Columbia, from the mountaintops to the saltwater's edge. But while much of the continent lay buried under hundreds of feet of ice and snow, large parts of what is now central Alaska and Yukon remained glacier-free grasslands. And at the same time, a land bridge crossed what is today the Bering Sea, connecting the Asian plains with the North American grasslands.

Those arid grasslands, with animal life plentiful enough to attract Asian hunters over the Bering land bridge, provided an entry for what may have been the continent's first North Americans. Then, somewhat more than 12,000 years ago, the glaciers began to recede, eventually opening an ice-free corridor east of the Rocky Mountains and leading south to the land beyond. Slowly, people from the North began to trickle south into new hunting grounds. Within a few thousand years their descendants would populate two continents.

It's possible the first groups to arrive on today's British Columbia seashore migrated from the coast of Alaska after ocean levels stabilized about 6,000 years ago. A more likely explanation, however, is that the first British Columbians came from the east somewhat earlier, following rivers and streams leading from the British Columbia interior to saltwater as the glaciers melted.

On the coast these early British Columbians found themselves in a mild climate rich with salmon, shellfish and other foods from the sea. About 4,000 years ago cedar became a significant part of the coastal forest, and it, too, became an increasingly important resource in the economic and cultural life of the coastal peoples. Because of the abundance of resources here, Indian people along the northwest coast spent more time in leisure and cultural pursuits. Because the food supply was abundant and dependable, the rich cultural life of these early West Coast communities was incredibly stable. For the most part, people on the coast lived in much the same way for 3,000 or even 4,000 years. Then three or four centuries ago, European explorers and traders began to make their first incursions.

Although Captain James Cook has long been heralded as the first European to set foot on what is today the British Columbia coast, it now seems likely that Sir Francis Drake visited the region 200 years earlier. Drake sailed north along the coast of North America during the summer of 1579, searching for a western entrance to what was imagined to be the Northwest Passage across the top of the continent. Sailing his ship, the *Golden Hind,* into the Strait of Juan de Fuca and some distance up the Strait of Georgia, Drake became convinced he had found the fabled passage. Since the route was presumed to be plagued with ice during all but the summer months and the weather was already cold and rainy, Drake decided to turn back into the open Pacific. He continued westward on a route that eventually took him back to England, thereby completing the historic first English circumnavigation of the world.

Once back in London, Drake, following orders from Queen

Elizabeth I, conspired to keep his supposed discovery of the Northwest Passage a secret. Drake and the queen wanted to prevent the news from reaching Spain, England's imperial competitor. The conspiracy worked well enough to obscure Drake's roll in the exploration of the northwest coast, but it had no real effect upon subsequent events in the region.

In 1588, while Drake was helping to defeat the Spanish Armada in Europe, Thomas Cavendish attempted to retrace Drake's route in the Pacific. After pillaging a Spanish galleon near Baja, California, Cavendish divided the loot between his two ships, then set sail across the Pacific in one vessel while sending the other north in an attempt to reach England through Drake's Northwest Passage. Not surprisingly, since there was no passage, the second ship was never heard from again.

Cavendish, however, inadvertently played a minor role in the future mapping of the northwest coast. During one of his encounters with the Spanish, he captured Juan de Fuca, whose real name was Apostolos Valerianos, a Greek sailing officer in the service of Spain. Cavendish held de Fuca captive for a time before eventually putting him ashore on the California coast. Years later, back in Europe, Juan de Fuca used information learned while Drake's captive to invent an imaginary voyage in which he claimed to have discovered, in 1592, what we now call the Strait of Juan de Fuca. At least, most historians believe de Fuca made up the voyage since it seems doubtful he or anyone else ever sailed a Spanish ship into the region at that time. The location and description he gave for the strait are amazingly accurate, however, and stranger tales have turned out to be true.

Even with de Fuca's tale, exploration of the far northwest coast halted for another 150 years until Russian traders began expanding their operations in Alaska. The Russians had barely established themselves on the Alaska shore by the second half of the eighteenth century, and no traders had even reached the northern part of what would become British Columbia, but their presence ignited Spanish fears in Mexico. Although Spain had never sent ships north of California, it had long declared ownership of the entire Pacific coast. To protect its tenuous interests, the governor of Mexico in San Blas sent ships north to find out what the Russians were up to and to fortify the meager Spanish claims in the region.

In June 1774, Juan Josef Perez Hernandez sailed the *Santiago* from San Blas, Mexico, with orders to claim territory and establish contacts with native people as far as 60° north latitude. Intimidated by the increasingly treacherous weather and perhaps the rocky shores and dangerous tides of the Inside Passage off southeastern Alaska, Perez turned back near the 55th parallel. His only contact with coastal Indians came on his return journey, when his men traded with Haida off the Queen Charlotte Islands and with the Nootka of Vancouver Island. Both groups canoed out to greet and trade with the Europeans, but on both occasions the timid Perez failed to go ashore.

The following year the Spanish sent the *Santiago* north once more, this time captained by Bruno de Hezeta and accompanied by a smaller craft, the *Sonora,* under the command of Juan Francisco de la Bodega y Quadra. Hezeta traveled only as far as the southern tip of Vancouver Island before turning back, but Quadra, in the 36-foot (11-m) *Sonora,* sailed north to the 57th parallel, where he erected a cross in today's Alaska Panhandle. Here, he declared all of the North American Northwest to be Spanish territory. Content with this symbolic gesture, Spain would not venture north again for nearly a decade.

Three years after Quadra's visit, Captain James Cook made the first authenticated European landing on what would become the British Columbia shore. Storms kept Cook too far out to sea to enter the Strait of Juan de Fuca or even realize it was there. But on March 29, 1778, his ship sailed into Nootka Sound, where, just as they had done during Perez's visit four years earlier, the Nootka rowed out in canoes to greet and trade with the European visitors. Cook spent only four weeks at Nootka before continuing his voyage of exploration north to Alaska and then south to Hawaii. There Cook was killed in a needless dispute with the Hawaiian king.

Cook's short stay at Nootka, however, was to have major commercial consequences. Because Cook intended to keep traveling north before turning back for Hawaii, he and many of his men exchanged a few European tools and trinkets with the Nootka for fur robes, mostly sea otter skins, to use as coats and bed clothes in the colder Alaskan waters. On the voyage home Cook's ships stopped in China, where the thick, greasy sea otter skins brought surprisingly high prices. For the first time, Englishmen realized that Russian traders were making huge fortunes in the Orient selling North American furs.

Word got around. In April 1785, Captain James Hanna, an English merchant involved in the China trade, became the first English trader to enter the Pacific fur trade when he sailed into Nootka Sound on Vancouver Island. Unfortunately, his visit also marked the first violent clash between Europeans and the Nootka people. Evidently, the fracas started when some of Hanna's sailors exploded gun powder under the chair of Nootka Chief Maquinna. The sailors claimed the incident was merely a joke, but the result was a quick and bloody fight in which several Nootka were killed. Hanna was able to smooth over relations with the Indians sufficiently to sail away with a shipload of sea otter furs.

By the following year, when Hanna returned for more, several rival traders had already been welcomed by the Nootka. In 1788, John Meares, another trader involved in the China trade, came to Vancouver Island and built a fur trading post at Nootka. This small establishment was the first European-style building in the Northwest. Meares had obtained permission to build on the site from Maquinna. But, given Nootka traditions regarding ownership of land, it's probable that the two men had a completely different understanding of the deal they made.

Meares also brought the first immigrants to Vancouver Island, about 70 Chinese laborers who came to work for Meares. Although Meares was trying to become the region's dominant fur trader, he was far from the only one. In addition to other English traders, the first Americans had also started operating on the northwest coast by this time. And in the spring of 1789, the Spanish also returned to Nootka.

While Meares was away selling furs in China, two Spanish vessels sailed into Nootka Sound under the command of Estaban Jose Martinez, who once more claimed the entire northwest coast for Spain. Citing the right of prior discovery, Martinez confiscated all of Meares' property, including the first sailing vessel built in what would become the Province of British Columbia, the *North West America*. Martinez also conscripted Meares' Chinese laborers into service for Spain, dismantled the English trader's store and built a somewhat more elaborate headquarters for himself. In succeeding months other Spanish ships, both officially and unofficially, came north to explore the British Columbia coast.

When news of Spain's seizure of Nootka reached Meares in

China, he immediately left for London to take his grievance against the Spanish to the English government. After hearing his story, parliament voted funds for England to prepare for a fight with Spain. However, negotiations prevailed when the first Nootka Convention of October 1790 was adopted. Under terms of the agreement, Meares was generously compensated for his losses and an uneasy accommodation for each country was negotiated.

These negotiations brought the West Coast's two most famous explorers back to the region. By the early summer of 1792, Captain George Vancouver and Juan Francisco de la Bodega y Quadra were cooperatively exploring and mapping the coast. At the same time, the two men tried to negotiate the best possible political solution for each of their countries in the region. Vancouver and Quadra became friends but weren't as successful at negotiating. Finally, a 1793 treaty declared that Spain and England would share Nootka and the Northwest, and that both would work together to keep other nations out. But in reality Spain's imperial presence in North America was already on the wane. Unable even to maintain areas already under her sole control, Spain ordered her last ship stationed in Nootka to leave in 1795, and Spain was never again a political factor in British Columbia.

With Spain out of the picture, Britain became the dominant force along the entire northwest coast from the Columbia River to Russian-occupied Alaska. Even while Vancouver was still mapping the west coast Alexander Mackenzie arrived in the area after crossing the continent from the east. This journey, which he took more than a decade before Lewis and Clark crossed the American plains, made Mackenzie the first white explorer to cross North America north of Mexico.

Mackenzie arrived on the coast when competition was intensifying between British North America's two major fur trading companies, the Hudson's Bay Company and the North West Company. Other trader explorers soon followed Mackenzie. Simon Fraser crossed the mountains to the northern interior in 1805. David Thompson crossed into the Kootenays in 1806. In 1808, Fraser followed the river that today bears his name all the way to the coast, and in 1811, Thompson followed another river to the coast, arriving at the mouth of the Columbia River only a few weeks after American traders had arrived by sea to build Fort Astoria. Two years later, during the War of 1812, Thompson's

Fort Victoria, circa 1860.

North West Company would buy that Columbia River post from the Americans.

In 1821, the North West Company was absorbed by its older competitor, and for nearly 50 years, the Hudson's Bay Company wielded British power in the Northwest. Treaties had by then confirmed that Russia and Spain were confined to defined areas to the north and south. Only Britain and the United States were left to maintain an uneasy shared accommodation in the middle Northwest. In 1846, the Oregon Boundary Treaty finally established a permanent border along the 49th parallel from the Rocky Mountains to the Pacific. At the ocean the boundary dipped below Vancouver Island, eventually dividing the southernmost Gulf Islands, where the border extended from Point Roberts to the middle of the Strait of Juan de Fuca.

Three years before the boundary treaty was signed, Chief Factor James Douglas of the Hudson's Bay Company had established Fort Victoria on the southern tip of Vancouver Island. The new fort had been built as a trade and supply point that would stand well north of the Columbia River, where company officials hoped the American boundary would be drawn. Douglas, Chief Factor James McLoughlin and company Governor George Simpson also deemed Vancouver Island a prudent choice for the company headquarters. They knew that because the Americans wanted access to Puget Sound, there was a good chance the boundary would be settled farther north than historic occupation would otherwise dictate. Once the boundary was established at the 49th parallel, the Hudson's Bay Company began moving its operations to Fort Victoria and slowly selling off its southern assets, including Fort Vancouver, its long-established company headquarters on the Columbia.

By 1849, when Hudson's Bay Company's headquarters formally moved to Fort Victoria, James Douglas already knew the fort was about to become the capital of the new colony of Vancouver Island, but he had no way of knowing that the gold discovered that year in California would also soon begin to change his tiny outpost into a trading center for the entire Northwest. He had no idea that within the decade the discovery of more gold would turn his tiny settlement on the edge of a still mostly unknown wilderness into a gold rush boomtown. And he had no way to know that in little more than two decades the site of his fort would become a provincial capital in a country, Canada, that did not yet exist. Certainly Douglas could never have begun to imagine the city that occupies that place today or any of the towns and cities that now dot what he considered a mostly forbidding and desolate coastal wilderness.

Chapter 1

Victoria and the South Island

Victoria, Port Renfrew and
the Saanich Peninsula

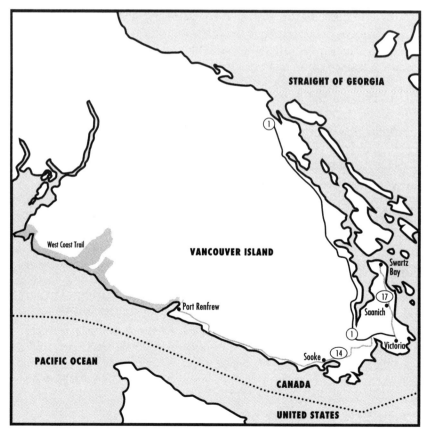

VICTORIA—with its pleasant climate, sheltered harbor, sidewalk cafés and bustling tourist shops—radiates exuberance and charm. Almost everywhere in downtown Victoria, history buffs can stroll past buildings still in use after a century and more. They can walk through Chinatown's historic Fan Tan Alley, visit the Provincial Museum and have a picnic in Beacon Hill Park near where James Douglas of the Hudson's Bay Company first came ashore in 1842. Certainly, Victoria is a delightful place for anyone interested in North America's pioneering past. The city's busy downtown is lined with streets named after people from its early years as a fur post and gold rush town. Building after building along many of these streets dates from before or soon after the turn of the century. The legislative buildings on the harbor's edge were built in the 1890s. Across the street, the Empress Hotel, constructed just after the turn of the century, exaggerates the city's British heritage as ostentatiously as the busy, double-decker English tour buses that wait for tourists out front. Chinatown, Bastion Square (where the old jail is now a museum) and a multitude of other heritage buildings all speak of an exciting and memorable past.

A large totem pole collection featuring works from several coastal tribes can be found near the Royal British Columbia Provincial Museum at Thunderbird Park. The museum itself includes extensive coastal aboriginal exhibits. The Helmcken House, built in 1852 and now Victoria's oldest historic home open to the public, can be found on the grounds near the museum. Other early residences still standing in Victoria include artist Emily Carr's home, dating from 1863, and the Point Ellice House, built in 1861 by the colony's first gold commissioner, Peter O'Reilly.

Across southern Vancouver Island, from the Saanich Peninsula to Port Renfrew, a multitude of historical artifacts and anecdotes wait to be discovered by any traveler willing to look. Drive along the ocean at Cadboro Bay, where a large Salish Indian village had already stood for hundreds of years when Fort Victoria was just being built. Drive up the Saanich Peninsula along Veyaness Road (V & S), the route where the original Victoria and Sidney Railway once ran. Cross the bridge in downtown Victoria to Esquimalt and its historic harbor, then drive along the Strait of Juan de Fuca to the end of the road at Port Renfrew. Everywhere there are places to explore southern Vancouver Island's exciting history.

Beacon Hill Becomes British Columbia's First Park
Beacon Hill Park, western end of Trans–Canada Highway, Douglas Street at Dallas Road, Victoria

Beacon Hill Park became British Columbia's first public park in the 1850s, when the Hudson's Bay Company set aside land here for public use. The site had already been used as an unofficial gathering place for citizens almost as long as Fort Victoria had been in existence. Its name comes from the beacon fires that were built here during the early years of the fort on the large hill overlooking the Strait of Juan de Fuca. The fires warned approaching ships of Brotchie Ledge, a submerged reef just offshore named after Captain William Brotchie, who sailed the barque *Albion* against the reef in 1849. Brotchie Ledge caused several other wrecks before officials began using the fire beacons in the early 1850s.

James Douglas, superintendent for the Hudson's Bay Company in the region and the first governor of Vancouver Island, was particularly fond of Beacon Hill. He first visited the site in the early 1840s on an early voyage to southern Vancouver Island to scout locations for a new fur post. On the day in 1843 when he chose a spot for the new Fort Victoria, he came ashore at Clover Point along the shore east of Beacon Hill and then walked through today's park before crossing to the inner harbor. Earlier, Douglas had described the area to Hudson's Bay Company officials as "a perfect Eden in the midst of the dreary wilderness of the northwest coast, and so different in its general aspect from the wooded, rugged regions around that one might be dropped from the clouds into its present position."

Richard Blanshard Becomes First Island Governor in Name Only
Blanshard Street, Victoria

In 1849, after the border with the United States had been officially set at the 49th parallel, the British government decided it would be prudent to establish Vancouver Island as a crown colony and thus stave off any future American expansion in the area. Despite the noble plan, however, the British government actually wanted as little to do with far-off Vancouver Island as possible, especially if it meant spending money. As a result the British colonial presence on Vancouver Island was halfhearted at best.

Although the island was technically a colony, the government turned almost everything over to the Hudson's Bay Company. All the island's land, more than 12,000 square miles (31,078 square km), was leased to the company for the picayune sum of seven shillings a year (about $1.50). In return the Hudson's Bay Company was obliged to try to make Vancouver Island a true colonial outpost. The most onerous of its tasks, as the company saw it, was the requirement that it encourage settlement.

The Hudson's Bay Company, of course, preferred to keep the island for itself. Settlers, unless they were loyal employees, had already proven to be a nuisance in other places under the domain of the fur company. They interfered with the pursuit of profits, and, as had been the case in the Oregon Territory and the Manitoba Red River region, they were often downright rebellious. Still, if there had to be settlers in order for the company to gain control of Vancouver Island, so be it. The solution for James Douglas and other company officials was to accept the obligation, but make settling on Vancouver Island so unattractive that few would attempt it. The easiest way to do this was to make land prices high for everyone except retiring employees of the Hudson's Bay Company. This immediately became company policy in the new colony.

A true colony, of course, needed a governor. But there just weren't many suitable candidates willing to travel to the other side of the world in order to govern a colony viewed in the mother country as a desolate outpost, where the only residents were a handful of fur traders and a native population yet to be subjugated.

The task of finding a governor was made even more difficult because the position was unpaid and included none of the perks usually associated with crown colony governorships. Vancouver Island's land had already gone to the Hudson's Bay Company, so there were no large grants of land to be made for a governor's personal enrichment. There were no servants, no government employees to oversee and no lavish official residence. There certainly was no standing army waiting at a governor's command. In fact, for a governor in far-off Vancouver Island, there were no duties of any kind that might bring prestige back home in England. In fact, there was almost nothing worth bothering about under his charge on the island itself. There were virtually no settlers, and the Hudson's Bay Company held all the real power.

Surprisingly, however, the British government was able to find its man. Richard Blanshard, for whom Blanshard Street in Victoria is now named, was so anxious to get his foot in the door of government service that he undertook to travel around the southern tip of South America and up the coast of both Americas to Fort Victoria at his own expense. He arrived on March 9, 1850, during a dismal and particularly rainy spring. He had been nearly six months at sea by the time he arrived, but once at Victoria he found that the Hudson's Bay Company hadn't even gotten around to building him a house. Blanshard was forced to stay aboard the HMS *Diver,* the sailing ship that had brought him from England, until other accommodations could be arranged. For a time the government of the new colony, in the person of Richard Blanshard, went everywhere the *Diver* did as it sailed along the Vancouver Island shore. Eventually, Blanshard moved into a clerk's quarters at Fort Victoria and then into a residence of his own when the company finally had it built.

As a young English barrister, Blanshard had no experience as an administrator, but it mattered little since there was very little for him to administer. The colony had virtually no people, no money, no taxes and no government officials to carry out official duties. For Douglas and the Hudson's Bay Company, who were pleased to remain unhindered by government interference, it was a perfect arrangement.

Not long after he arrived, however, even Richard Blanshard realized he could never hope to be anything but a figurehead governor on Vancouver Island. In November, nine frustrating months after his arrival, Blanshard sent a letter of resignation to England. He departed for that country himself as soon as he received word that his resignation had been accepted. The English government then appointed James Douglas as the new governor. Douglas, of course, already ruled Vancouver Island and most of what is now mainland British Columbia as the Hudson's Bay Company's highest ranking officer in the region. The British government had simply confirmed in name what was already true in fact.

James Douglas Governs Two Colonies
Douglas Street, Victoria

For over eight years—seven of them as colonial governor—James Douglas, who gave his name to Douglas Street in downtown Victoria, ruled Vancouver Island as an arm of the Hudson's Bay Company. A more diverse commerce developed on Vancouver Island than was usually the case in the fur industry, but the population remained small, and Douglas was allowed to manage most of the region's affairs as he saw fit. For Douglas, the public good and the good of the Hudson's Bay Company were one and the same. But when gold was discovered in 1858 along the Fraser River on the British Columbia mainland, everything changed—almost overnight.

Victoria's population, which had been about 200 at the beginning of the year, jumped to 5,000 as an estimated 30,000 prospectors passed through town in the spring and summer on their way to the gold fields of the Fraser. Most used the fort and new town springing up around it as a stopping-off place on their way to the mainland. Others came to set up businesses that would cater to the prospectors passing through. Most of the new arrivals were Americans, but many were eastern Canadians, Europeans and Chinese.

Douglas knew immediately that the old ways of ruling Vancouver Island were over. Never again would the Hudson's Bay Company be able to dictate public policy. But Douglas's immediate problem was that while he was the British governor for Vancouver Island, he had no official status on the mainland, where thousands of prospectors were moving. The territory had been ceded to the Hudson's Bay Company for the fur trade, but the British government had never bothered to make the area a colony. With few Europeans in the region, the bother and expense of establishing official government institutions seemed unnecessary.

Douglas didn't let the fact that he had no real authority stop him. He went about issuing mining regulations and attempting to bring order to the chaos that attended the huge influx of miners. In Britain, parliament hurriedly created the Colony of British Columbia and named James Douglas the governor of the new colony as well. Although the appointment stipulated that Douglas had to resign from his position with the Hudson's

James Douglas, Hudson's Bay Company chief factor and governor of the colonies of Vancouver Island and British Columbia.

Bay Company, the aging chief factor knew the old days of the fur trade were over anyway. He accepted his new position after first demanding £5,000 per year salary instead of the £1,000 offered, and then went on to rule both colonies, with the assistance of partly elected councils, for the next five years. Douglas retired in 1864 and continued to live in Victoria until his death in 1877.

Amelia Douglas Saves Husband's Life
Douglas Street, Victoria

Amelia Douglas, who, as the new wife of the young James Douglas, saved the future governor from an Indian attack in British Columbia's interior.

James Douglas, as governor of the colonies of Vancouver Island and British Columbia, was the most prominent and powerful man in the growing colonial outpost of Victoria. But his wife, Amelia, was ostracized for her Indian ancestry by its snob-bish, anglophone society. Amelia, the half-Cree daughter of a fur trader, had married Douglas while she was still a teenager and he a young man starting out in the fur trade at Fort St. James.

Once, Amelia even saved Douglas's life. The incident began after Douglas heard that an Indian named Tzil-na-o-lay, who had reportedly killed two Hudson's Bay Company employees, was liv-ing at the home of a Carrier chief near the fort. In accordance with company policy at the time, Douglas and some other Hud-son's Bay employees found and killed Tzil-na-o-lay for his alleged deeds. Not surprisingly, this angered other Carrier people, espe-cially the chief in whose home the murder had taken place.

The Indians swarmed Fort St. James in retaliation and cap-tured Douglas, who had directed the execution. Holding a knife to the young fur trader's heart, they were about to take their revenge when Amelia intervened. Familiar with the ways of her aboriginal cousins, she called for the Carrier chief to accept gifts in exchange for Tzil-na-o-lay's life rather than taking the life of her husband in retribution. The Indians delayed the execution while Amelia and the other women of the fort began bringing out trade goods. When the pile reached a sufficient level, Dou-glas's life was spared.

Afterward, however, Hudson's Bay Company officials decid-ed that Indian resentment against the young Douglas ran so high that it wasn't safe for him to remain in the North. In 1830, the company transferred him to its headquarters on the Colum-bia River far to the south. It was here, as the new fort accountant, that Douglas began his rise to power in the Hudson's Bay Com-pany and eventually in the colonies of Vancouver Island and British Columbia.

Finlayson Blows Up Songhee Lodge
Finlayson Street, Victoria

Only a year after the founding of Fort Victoria, a test of wills developed between Tzouhalem, one of the most feared Indian leaders on the south coast, and Roderick Finlayson, the newly appointed 26-year-old commander of the Hudson's Bay fur post. Tzouhalem was a Cowichan from the east coast of Vancouver Island. He was known throughout the region to white and Indi-

Old Hudson's Bay Company bastion at corner of View and Government streets, prior to its demolition in December 1860.

an alike for his ferocity and fearlessness. He particularly resented whites for their encroachment on Indian lands. Long before the founding of Fort Victoria, Tzouhalem had traveled across the Strait of Georgia to the Fraser River, where he attempted to shoot the commander at Fort Langley and scare whites from the area.

When Tzouhalem heard about the establishment of Fort Victoria, he decided to pay a similar visit to the newest white arrivals on the British Columbia coast. Late in the summer of 1844, Tzouhalem led a band of his warriors to the Songhee village that had recently been built near the new fort. Tzouhalem had long terrorized the Songhee, and he knew Tsil-al-thach, the chief there, might well fight the whites. When he arrived, however, Tsil-al-thach was away, so Tzouhalem walked into the village and assumed command. One of his first orders was for hunters to shoot some of the cattle grazing near the fort so he could taste the meat.

When Finlayson found out that the cattle and several horses had been killed, he closed the fort's gate and sent a message to Tzouhalem. Finlayson demanded the surrender of the men who had killed the animals and payment for the livestock. Tzouhalem replied that the land and all the animals that grazed upon it belonged to the Indians. In retaliation, Finlayson immediately suspended all trade with the Indians; Tzouhalem then sent for more of his Cowichan warriors and began planning an attack on the fort.

Soon, the Indians began shooting, riddling the fort's stockade with musket balls for half an hour. Finlayson told his men to hold their fire. After the Indian volley halted, the young commander sent out his interpreter. Pretending to have escaped from the fort, the interpreter told the Indians to get everyone out of a prominent lodge that stood near the center of the village. Finlayson, he said, was preparing to destroy it with cannon fire. The lodge quickly emptied, and Finlayson, relying on a prearranged signal from his interpreter, aimed a nine-pound cannon loaded with grape shot and fired.

Cedar boards flew into the air, splintering and falling to the ground. With one shot, Finlayson had destroyed the building. Indians scattered in fear, and soon a number of lesser chiefs returned to the fort to ask for peace. Finlayson demanded that either the men who had killed the cattle be surrendered or payment be made in furs equal to the livestock's value. Within a few minutes payment was made.

Tzouhalem, however, was not convinced that the white men could destroy the village. The next day a group of Songhees went to Finlayson and asked to see another example of the cannon's power. Finlayson told the Indians to push an empty canoe into the harbor in front of the fort. When the canoe was in place, Finlayson shot a cannon ball, and the canoe exploded from the water with splintered cedar flying. The cannon ball, after ripping through the canoe, continued on, skipping across the harbor like a flat stone until it reached the opposite shore, where it sailed into the woods and disappeared.

After this, Tzouhalem and his warriors left the Songhee village and returned to Cowichan Bay. A few weeks later Finlayson decided to move the Songhee village across the harbor, where the Indians would pose less of a threat to the fort. Initially, the Songhee protested. But remembering the destruction wielded by the white men's cannon and after demanding that the traders help dismantle their village and rebuild it on the opposite shore, the Indians moved their houses as they had been told. As for Tzouhalem, he continued to instill fear in the hearts of whites and Indians alike for another 10 years. Then in 1854, he was killed by Indians on Kuper Island while he was attempting to kidnap a woman he intended to force into slavery.

Birdcages Built to Hold Politicians
Legislative Buildings, Victoria Harbour, Victoria

The British Columbia legislative buildings in downtown Victoria took four years to build and opened in 1897 just as the Klondike Gold Rush was getting underway. The grandiose seat of government, built from British Columbia granite from Haddington Island at a cost of nearly $1 million, replaced more modest headquarters originally built by the colonial government.

The original buildings, constructed between 1859 and 1862 in the same area as the present provincial government headquarters, replaced the colonial legislative council meeting place—a spare room in the aging Fort Victoria. The buildings reflected the period's architectural penchant for oriental styles. People said the pagoda roofs and crisscrossed bright, red-lacquered woodwork made the buildings resemble birdcages, and that name became the universal appellation given to the seat of government here, colonial and provincial, until the present buildings opened.

Architect Murdered after Cheating on Wife
Legislative Buildings and Empress Hotel, Victoria Harbour, Victoria

What may be the two most photographed buildings in British Columbia, the provincial legislative building and the Empress Hotel, stand catercorner from each other by the harbor in downtown Victoria. Both were designed by the same architect, Francis Mawson Rattenbury. Rattenbury came to Victoria in 1892 hoping to win the contract to design and build the proposed new legislature. A few months after the buildings opened, the successful architect married Florence Nunn, daughter of a retired, socially prominent British army captain.

Rattenbury and his bride left Victoria almost immediately after the wedding, bound for the Klondike, where Rattenbury harbored a misguided notion of making a fortune running riverboats on the Yukon River. His scheme was sunk before it got started, and the couple soon found themselves back in Victoria, where Rattenbury settled into life as the province's most renowned architect.

Beginning in 1923, however, Rattenbury became romantically entangled with Alma Pakenham, an already twice-married Vic-

The Birdcages, British Columbia's first parliament buildings.

toria piano teacher 30 years his junior. In the small-town atmosphere of Victoria, the affair soon became public knowledge, and Rattenbury and his paramour found themselves ostracized. For two years Florence held out against a divorce, and even when she finally consented in 1925, Rattenbury found himself something of an outcast among Victoria's version of high society. His architectural business in shambles, he and Alma married and moved to England in 1929. Six years later Rattenbury was murdered by his chauffeur, who had become Alma's new lover.

Father of Oregon Establishes Victoria
McLoughlin Point, Victoria Harbour, Victoria

Dr. John McLoughlin, the Hudson's Bay Company chief factor, became known as the Father of Oregon for the encouragement he provided to the territory's early settlers. He also was responsible for the founding of Fort Victoria in 1842. McLoughlin, a tall, imposing man with a shock of white hair, was born in Rivière du Loop, Quebec. He studied medicine in Europe, and after returning to Canada he became a doctor for the North West Company. McLoughlin showed an aptitude for the business side of fur trading early in his career, and he was soon recognized more as a trader than healer.

John McLoughlin, the Hudson's Bay Company chief factor at Fort Vancouver from 1824 to 1846.

Posted at Fort William on the northwest shore of Lake Superior, McLoughlin began to take on commercial as well as medical duties. Eventually, he was appointed a chief trader for the company. Then in 1823, after the amalgamation of the North West and Hudson's Bay companies, McLoughlin was appointed to direct the fur company's operations over the entire Columbia district. Initially, McLoughlin based his operations out of Fort

George (formally Fort Astoria) on the Pacific coast at the mouth of the Columbia River, but he soon moved his headquarters up the Columbia to the newly built Fort Vancouver on the river's north side.

It was at Fort Vancouver, starting in the 1830s, that McLoughlin began his efforts to help newly arrived settlers, most of them American. Although the Hudson's Bay Company had traditionally been antagonistic to any settlement in its domain, especially by Americans, McLoughlin had strong republican leanings and sympathized with the settlers who had crossed the continent to begin a new life on its far western frontier. He extended credit to the Americans to help them through their initial years of struggle.

Perhaps it was McLoughlin's North American upbringing that was responsible for his democratic sympathies, or perhaps it was the socially rigid and autocratic Hudson's Bay Company itself. Whatever the cause, his contribution to the welfare of the American settlers was noticed by company officials, and he was eventually forced into retirement in 1846. McLoughlin then took up residence in Oregon City and became an American citizen. He died in 1857 with his contribution to the pioneers of the region largely unrecognized. Some of his neighbors were downright hostile toward McLoughlin because of his affiliation with the Hudson's Bay Company. It was left for later historians to record his contribution to the settling of the Oregon Territory.

Despite McLoughlin's sympathies for American settlers, he also was completely loyal to the Hudson's Bay Company, at least as he saw it. McLoughlin ruled all the land west of the Rocky Mountains, from the Spanish border to Russian Sitka. He was responsible for the founding of Fort Simpson near today's Prince Rupert, Fort McLoughlin at Bella Bella and Fort Victoria on the southern tip of Vancouver Island. Ironically, McLoughlin's desire to establish Fort Victoria stemmed from his realization that the scores of Oregon immigrants he had helped settle in the region also bolstered American claims to the territory. By 1842, McLoughlin understood that the large American settlement in the area might one day be enough to cause the international border to be declared farther north than he had ever imagined possible when he had first arrived in what was then a lone British outpost on the western edge of the continent.

Butt Kicked Out of Victoria
Government and Yates Streets, Victoria

John Butts, or John Butt as he was universally known in Victoria, has to qualify as one of the city's most colorful characters of the gold rush era. Butt left his native England for California in the mid-1850s, a few years too late for that gold rush. In San Francisco he was implicated in a murder and imprisoned for a time by the local vigilante committee. Freed in 1858, he headed north to Victoria to join the Fraser River Gold Rush. He never made that one, either. Instead of continuing to the diggings on the mainland, Butt settled down to a job in Victoria as the city's first and last town crier.

The diminutive Butt was instructed to stand on prominent street corners and ring a huge, wooden-handled bell to gain people's attention. After that he was to read out local news of auction sales, social events, theatrical performances, government proclamations and other matters of public concern. He also was directed to conclude each of his readings with the invocation "God Save the Queen." Sometimes Butt did as he was told. But more often than not he would end his reading, then glance furtively about to see if any magistrate or government official was within earshot. If not, he would conclude his remarks with the invocation "God save John Butt." In due course this matter was brought to the attention of government officials, and Butt was promptly dismissed.

It wasn't long before Butt found a new position: free-lance street cleaner for downtown merchants. With horse and cart he would collect litter and garbage on, say, Government Street and then drive around the corner to Fort Street. There he would lift the cart tailgate slightly and drive off down the rough road at a pace that would deposit the collected refuse on that street.

Butt would then report to the merchants on Fort Street, offering to pick up their litter. He would subsequently collect and deposit the garbage back on Government Street. In this manner, for a number of weeks, Butt created what seemed to be a full-time job for himself. Eventually, of course, Butt's working habits were discovered, and once more he found himself unemployed.

At this point Butt apparently took up the illegal sale of whiskey to the aboriginal community, allegedly with a lucrative sideline in petty thievery. Occasionally, Butt even resorted to begging at back doors, singing for his supper in his famous town-crier voice.

After a time, of course, Butt's whiskey selling captured the attention of authorities, who had him imprisoned. Butt appeared unconcerned about going to jail, but he was upset when prison officials tried to put him to work on the chain gang. Almost immediately after he learned of his proposed duties, he suffered a strange attack of paralysis. The unusual illness left the poor man unable to move his feet or feel any pain in his legs below the knees. Malingering was suspected, but hot needles stabbed into his calves seemed to cause him no discomfort. Still skeptical, the authorities transferred Butt from prison to a local hospital. There, he was carried from his bed every day and placed in a chair at the front of the building, where he would sit in the sun and talk with visitors and staff as they carried on their business. Sometimes he would even sing for everyone.

Several times, though, it was reported that Butt had made a slight movement of his leg or foot while holding court in his chair. Doctors were brought in to observe from a distance. Then one morning after Butt had been carried to his chair, someone dumped a bucket of cold water on him from the verandah above. Butt evidenced an immediate and miraculous cure. He jumped from his chair in surprise, and after a second bucket of ice water landed on his head, he ran from the building like a sprinter.

After being captured and serving the rest of his jail time on the work gang, Butt found a job in the kitchen of the Colonial Hotel in Victoria. Soon afterward the hotel catered a tea meeting for one of Victoria's churches. Somehow, Butt managed to sur-reptitiously mix the contents of two bottles of brandy into the tea and coffee served at the affair. The effect on the devout crowd was everything he hoped it would be.

News of the event soon spread through Victoria, and the next morning Justice of the Peace De Courcy was standing on Government Street discussing the matter with passersby. While thus employed, De Courcy, with some disgust, noted that he'd give an entire pound sterling to learn the name of the man who had doctored the drinks. As fortune would have it, Butt was standing nearby at the time, and overhearing De Courcy's remarks, he said, "Hand over the pound, judge. I'm the man that did it."

Instead of handing over the money, however, De Courcy flew into a rage, grabbed Butt by the collar and began giving him a series of powerful kicks to his backside. Butt howled in agony, but still De Courcy kicked and cursed him until exhaustion ended the spontaneous application of punishment. Butt retreated to the far side of the street without waiting for the promised payment. Only a few weeks later, though, Butt was caught stealing a goose. Once again he was sentenced to the chain gang, but Governor Douglas pardoned the former town crier on the condition that he leave the city that afternoon aboard a boat departing for Australia. Butt accepted the offer and was never seen nor heard in Victoria again.

Newspaper Editor Runs for Office
Times-Colonist Building, 2621 Douglas Street, Victoria

Victoria's *Times-Colonist* newspaper started publication as the *British Colonist* in 1858. It was founded by Amor De Cosmos, an eccentric bachelor who had been born with the name William Alexander Smith in Nova Scotia and who went on in 1873 to become premier of the infant Province of British Columbia. Smith left Nova Scotia as a young man to join the California Gold Rush. Although he never did any actual prospecting, it was in the gold mining town of El Dorado that he changed his name to Amor De Cosmos. The name change, he said, was because he loved the universe so completely. Others said De Cosmos simply thought too highly of himself to be satisfied with a name as common as Bill Smith.

Whatever the reason for the change, Smith arrived in Victoria as Amor De Cosmos during the Fraser River Gold Rush and almost immediately threw himself into the political life of the booming gold rush city of Victoria. He started the *British Colonist* in that same year to give himself a public platform. De Cosmos, like most of the gold rush immigrants who bothered to concern themselves with such matters, pitted himself against the autocratic colonial government of Governor James Douglas and the de facto rule of the Hudson's Bay Company.

De Cosmos, with his scathing editorials, soon became the leader of the democratic movement on Vancouver Island. Day after day he claimed, with some justice, that participation in government on the island was restricted to a small core of men with ties of one sort or another to James Douglas and the Hudson's Bay Company. Douglas did little to appease the De Cosmos's reformers. Arrogantly, he wrote, "people do not naturally take much interest in affairs of government as long as affairs go on well and prosperously. . . . *Common people* are content to leave questions of state to their ruling classes."

The extent of Douglas's grip on the affairs of the colony is clear in his reaction to De Cosmos's early attempts to be elected to the colonial assembly. De Cosmos first ran for office in 1858. When it appeared he might win, the colonial government suddenly decided that black immigrants, who had fled slavery in the United States, were British citizens and could therefore vote, even though other American citizens who had immigrated to Victoria were not extended the same privilege. The logic was that since people couldn't possibly be considered citizens of a country that would enslave them, they must be citizens of the territory in which they resided. Blacks in Victoria at the time were, quite naturally, appreciative of the sanctuary they had found on Vancouver Island. Almost to a man, they supported Douglas and the ruling clique of Hudson's Bay men in the assembly. De Cosmos lost the election.

De Cosmos ran again in an Esquimalt by-election the next year. This time his opponent was a government member named G.T. Gordon. Public opinion, mostly from immigrants from eastern Canada, seemed to predict a De Cosmos victory. Again the colonial government resorted to extraordinary measures to ensure victory. Instead of the 1859 voter eligibility list, it used the preceding year's list, which prevented some of De Cosmos's friends from voting. The government also brought up the question of De Cosmos's new name in an attempt to bar him from office. Since De Cosmos had changed his name in California, they said, there was no such person as Amor De Cosmos anywhere in British territory. De Cosmos, of course, disagreed, but just to be on the safe side, he entered his name as "William Alexander Smith, commonly known as Amor De Cosmos."

Voting at this time was still conducted by voice. The election had proceeded to a 10–10 tie with only one more eligible voter yet to arrive, a man known to be a De Cosmos supporter. Time went by, with De Cosmos supporters beginning to suspect their voter had been waylaid. Then suddenly, just as the sheriff was about to declare the voting over, the man arrived. Somewhat flustered by his tardiness, he blurted out that his vote was for Amor De Cosmos. The sheriff, who of course had gained his position by appointment from Governor Douglas, noted the vote, closed the polls and declared Gordon the winner. The vote, according to the sheriff, was 10 votes for Alexander Smith, 10 votes for Gordon and one for Amor De Cosmos. Since Smith and Gordon were tied, the sheriff himself broke the manufactured deadlock with a vote for Gordon. Once more, De Cosmos was thwarted.

But Douglas could not stem the democratic tide forever. Two years later, on his third try, De Cosmos succeeded. Later, the same year, James Douglas retired as colonial governor. De Cosmos went on to lead the reform group in the colonial assembly. He also pressed for confederation with the new country of Canada, a goal reached in 1870. In 1873, while serving simultaneously in the British Columbia legislature and the Canadian parliament, Amor De Cosmos became the second premier of British Columbia.

Dunsmuir Dies Building Castle
1050 Joan Crescent, Victoria

Robert Dunsmuir came from Scotland to British Columbia with his family in order to mine coal for the Hudson's Bay Company. He talked his wife into joining him by promising her that one day he would build her a castle.

In 1855, miners went on strike against the Hudson's Bay Company, but Dunsmuir refused to participate. As a reward the company gave him a free-miner's license after the strike was settled, and he began working an abandoned coal seam for himself. Eventually, Dunsmuir became a mine manager for other companies as well. He also continued prospecting for more lucrative coal deposits on his own. By the early 1870s, he had founded his own company, and his exploration work had yielded some of the highest grade coal deposits in the Northwest.

From that time on, his coal and almost everything else Dunsmuir touched seemed to turn to gold. By 1880, his company produced more coal than any other in British Columbia. Within another two years he had managed to buy out all his nonfamily partners in his mining ventures. Then he orchestrated the building of the Esquimalt and Nanaimo Railway. It was not only profitable, but also gave Dunsmuir and his new partners, who included his two sons, land grants totaling one-fifth of Vancouver Island. That land grant gave him control of all the likely coal-producing areas on the eastern side of the island.

By the late 1880s, Dunsmuir, who was probably the richest man in British Columbia, was ready to retire. Remembering his old promise to build his wife a Scottish castle, he ordered the construction of Craigdarroch Castle, an imposing four-story, turreted stone building that remains standing in Victoria. Dunsmuir never lived here, however. As the building was nearing completion, he died.

Chinatown Divided from Victoria by More than Ravine
Chinatown, Fisgaard Street, Victoria

Market Square in today's downtown Victoria is built over a site where a ravine once divided Chinatown from the rest of the growing city. A sometimes seasonal stream that flowed through the ravine supplied water for many city residents. Later, it was used as a garbage dump.

The city's first Chinese residents came during the Fraser River Gold Rush in 1858, and the first buildings on the north side of the ravine were constructed about this time. Many whites came to resent the Chinese population. Not only were many of the Chinese miners successful in the gold fields, they also developed a reputation for finding gold in places already worked over or explored unsuccessfully by white miners. Resentments also developed against the Chinese because many, unable to get better-paying jobs, worked for lower wages than generally earned by whites. Many whites felt this drove down wages for everyone.

By the 1890s, when the brick buildings that now form the north wall of Market Square were built, Victoria's Chinatown population was the largest in Canada, probably numbering well over 10,000 people. By this time the provincial government had passed laws forbidding Chinese citizens from acquiring crown land, and the federal government had passed legislation requiring Chinese immigrants to pay a head tax in order to enter the country. The policies were designed to drastically reduce the number of people emigrating from China. But since immigrants from that country continued to arrive, the government increased the tax steadily until, soon after the turn of the century, it reached the nearly prohibitive sum of $500.

About this same time Chinatown's opium factories—factories that had operated legally until then—were shut down. In 1908, Victoria barred children of Chinese descent born outside the country from attending public schools. Chinese citizens appealed to the Canadian courts for redress, but without success. As a result, Victoria's Chinese residents opened their own school, Zhonghua Xuetang, to provide their children with a basic education. Zhonghua Xuetang still teaches children in its building on Fisgaard Street in Chinatown. Today, though, with public schools open to all city children, Zhonghua Xuetang offers courses in Chinese languages and culture on Saturdays and after public school hours to children of any race, nationality or religion.

Fire Destroys Victoria's Red Light District
Government Street at Herald and Chatham, Victoria

Chatham and Herald streets between Government Street and the waterfront, in what was once the heart of Victoria's skid row district, were home to the city's red light area until the early 1900s. In the 1880s, the district here, known as the "restricted area," was the largest in the Northwest. Wide-spread sex slavery was an unpublicized aspect of the trade, and Victoria was probably a key port of entry for women and girls sold into prostitution in cities down the Pacific coast as far south as California.

Authorities largely ignored Victoria's red light area, leaving what policing there was to the bouncers employed in various saloons and bawdy houses. Newspapers or official records document little of life here during these years. Polite society at the end of the Victorian era held that such matters were unfit for public discussion and best ignored. There were other equally compelling reasons for the city's reluctance to confront the problems associated with the district. Foremost was the almost certain connection, both financial and personal, that many of Victoria's supposedly most upright citizens held to the area.

In the early days, when frontier Victoria was a mostly male settlement, several prominent citizens, who later went on to noteworthy careers in other fields, were known to have had financial dealings in the district. As well, many early prostitutes married into the community. Forever after, both they and their husbands tried to erase all memory of their past lives from the public record. As a consequence, it was usually deemed best in turn-of-the-century Victoria to never discuss matters about the "restricted area."

On July 23, 1907, a fire started in a blacksmith shop at the corner of Herald and Store streets. It swept through the red light district, destroying nearly 100 buildings and putting at least 250 people, almost all of them women, on the street. There is no record of any public response to the personal disasters resulting from the fire. No churches stepped forward to provide charity for the homeless or food for the destitute. No stories ran in local newspapers. Slowly, the area began to rebuild, but Victoria's citizens had quickly learned to appreciate the absence of the bawdy houses, and the area was closed down to the trade three years later.

Jemmy Jones Steals Own Boat
Fort Street (Cadboro Bay Road), Cadboro Bay, Victoria

If you follow Fort Street east from downtown Victoria to where it becomes Cadboro Bay Road, you eventually reach Cadboro Bay. A small island at the entrance of the bay is named for Jemmy Jones, one of most notorious sailors and smugglers in British Columbia history. Jones ran one of his vessels, the *Carolina*, aground on this island in the late 1850s.

Jemmy Jones had left his native Wales to look for gold in California in 1849, coming north to British Columbia during the Fraser River Gold Rush in 1856. Not long afterward he built a boat and entered the coastal trade, sailing between Vancouver Island, the Canadian mainland and nearby American communities. Before long, Jones developed a reputation for carrying on commerce in a way that appeared totally unencumbered by national or international trade laws. It was said that Jones had at one time or another been an involuntary guest in every coastal jail from San Francisco to Victoria, largely because of his tendency to skip out on his debts. Some said this wasn't done intentionally, but only because Jones never learned to read and write and so had to keep track of all his obligations in his head. Sometimes, or so his defenders said, he just forgot.

Jones' most famous exploit was an incident in 1865 when he stole his own boat and absconded with it to Mexico. Named for his wife, the boat was the *Jenny Jones*, built after the wreck of several previous Jones vessels. Originally a sailing vessel, the craft was fitted with steam engines and chugged between Oregon and British Columbia, with Port Townsend as its home port. The 1865 incident started in regular fashion with Jones being imprisoned in a Victoria jail for nonpayment of debt. This time, though, Jones escaped and paddled a getaway canoe across Juan de Fuca Strait.

Once on the American side, he found that his boat had been seized by an American marshal at Olympia in lieu of payment for another debt. Jones immediately made for the south shore of Puget Sound and, disguised as a woman, booked passage on his own boat. The *Jenny Jones* was bound for Seattle under charge of the local sheriff, where she was to be sold to pay off creditors. Arriving in Seattle that evening, the sheriff left a deputy in charge of watching the *Jenny Jones* and then retired to a Seattle hotel. The next morning, when the deputy went briefly ashore, Jones fired up the engines and steamed out of the harbor.

With only a sack of flour and a few other provisions on board, and with authorities from both Washington and British Columbia in hot pursuit, Jones headed north. At Port Ludlow he loaded enough firewood to push on to Nanaimo. There, he finagled additional food and hired a pair of Indians to dig coal for him at an old coal dump on Newcastle Island. Then Jones steamed off again, first to the mainland, where he picked up wood to burn with the poor quality coal, and then north again.

At Seymour Narrows, Jones fell in with the crew of a leaky sloop named the *Deerfoot,* which was loaded with trade goods and provisions. Jones managed to convince the men to abandon their sloop, join him and move the cargo and provisions to the *Jenny Jones.* Then Jones hurried off toward the top of Vancouver Island. There he rounded Cape Scott and headed for the open ocean. Twenty-five days later, Jones and his new crew landed at San Blas, Mexico, and immediately went into business. But plagued with a complaining crew, Jones soon sold his boat and headed north again.

In Seattle he was finally arrested for the theft his own boat. However, a sympathetic American judge threw the case out of court, claiming that the incident was at least indirectly the fault of the American sheriff who should have remained with the seized vessel. As it was, Jemmy Jones hadn't taken his ship from the sheriff, the judge explained, the sheriff had left Jemmy Jones with the ship. Thus freed, even if not exonerated, Jones headed back to Victoria, where he paid off enough of his debts to avoid jail. Within a short time he bought another boat and resumed trade on the Canadian coast.

Cadboro First to Explore Southern Vancouver Island
Cadboro Bay Road, Cadboro Bay, Victoria

Cadboro Bay is named after the Hudson's Bay Company brigantine *Cadboro,* which became, in 1842, the first European vessel to anchor here. Under the command of Captain Scarborough, the *Cadboro* was also the first ship to enter today's Victoria Harbour. And in 1827, the year the ship began its service on the northwest coast, it became the first Hudson's Bay vessel to enter the Fraser River. The *Cadboro* was eventually sold to private freighters in 1860. She was wrecked and sank in a heavy gale near Port Angeles in the Strait of Juan de Fuca on October 6, 1862.

Dismal Fly-Fishing Gives Part of British Columbia to Americans
Hillside Avenue at Cedar Hill Road, Victoria

For half a century, the west coast of British North America ran from the north shore of the Columbia River on today's Oregon–Washington border all the way north to Alaska. The United States began to assert ownership in the region after a large number of American settlers were allowed to settle there in the 1840s. In 1846, the British, despite earlier occupation and long use of the region, quietly bowed to American demands for the territory, and a treaty established the present international boundary along the 49th parallel.

The distant West Coast of North America was only a small, rather insignificant part of the British Empire at the time. Other

British interests, including getting along with the Americans in the Caribbean and other parts of the Atlantic, were of greater importance to the imperial government than this relatively small amount of real estate half a world away. The British government based its lack of interest on a report that concluded the territory in question was almost worthless anyway.

The report was written by Captain John Gordon of the British Frigate HMS *America*. Gordon spent part of the summer of 1845 examining the region for his brother, George Gordon, the British foreign minister at the time. According to Hudson's Bay Company officials, Gordon never even bothered exploring the Puget Sound area, sending several subservient officers in his place. As for Gordon, he spent most of his onshore time hunting and fly-fishing rather than exploring.

Gordon seems to have been a singularly unsuccessful sportsman in the Northwest, which did nothing to kindle his interest in the country. On one horseback hunt near Cedar Hill in today's Victoria, Gordon came across a large herd of deer. When he tried to chase the animals down as he would have done in Scotland, the deer simply escaped into thick brush nearby. After this disappointment, Gordon returned to the rod. Once again, however, he returned to the fort without success. "What a country, where salmon will not take the fly," he is reported to have told Governor Douglas. His assessment? Gordon said he "wouldn't trade the entire [northwest] coast for one Scottish hill."

The faraway British government, with little initial interest in the area and armed with Gordon's assessment of the territory, was happy enough in 1846 to unload the property on the Americans. They placed the international boundary at the 49th parallel instead of the Columbia River. Had the river boundary held, today's city of Vancouver, British Columbia, would have been 300 miles (483 km) south at Vancouver, Washington, where it would have been the capital of a much larger Province of British Columbia.

Hudson's Bay Company Farms Fail to Grow
Craigflower Manor, Highway 1 (Island Highway) at Admiral's Road, Victoria

---

During the 1800s, even the smallest Hudson's Bay Company trading posts usually planted some form of subsistence farm or garden. Growing your own took on added importance in the Northwest, however, because of the mild climate and the opportunities for trade that were created in produce. The Hudson's Bay Company, through its farming subsidiary, the Puget Sound Agricultural Company, established four major farming enterprises on southern Vancouver Island: Viewfield, Constance Cove, Colwood and Craigflower. None of the farms was particularly successful, however.

Constance Cove and Viewfield never amounted to much of anything. Viewfield was established in 1850, but after five years had only managed to clear 35 acres (14 ha) of its 600 acres (243 ha). By 1860, it had disappeared completely, with some of the farm having been sold and the rest simply abandoned. Constance Cove lasted five years longer, but then suffered essentially the same fate. For a time Colwood was more successful, with 200 acres (81 ha) cleared by 1855 and 30 families working the land. Nevertheless, it also failed under the dismal management of E.E. Langford, whose name graces the present community on Victoria's west side. Langford returned to England in 1861 after he was finally fired by the Hudson's Bay Company.

The last surviving farm, Craigflower, near Esquimalt Harbour, became the company's most successful farm on southern Vancouver Island. Craigflower was built under the direction of Kenneth McKenzie, a Hudson's Bay Company employee brought from England in 1854 to oversee the 24 families hired to work the farm. It grew grains, fruits and vegetables, and raised sheep, hogs, and dairy and beef cattle. McKenzie also ran a sawmill, flour mill, bakery, kilns, blacksmith forge and general store.

Perhaps McKenzie's greatest talent, however, was in the social rather than the agricultural field. During the 1850s and '60s, his home, Craigflower Manor, became one of Victoria's most popular gathering spots for the colonial outpost's social elite and visiting British naval officers putting in to nearby Esquimalt Harbour. Ultimately, however, although it was more enterprising than the other farms, Craigflower Farm managed to do only slightly better economically than the other company farms, and in 1866 it closed. Today, of the dozens of buildings that once stood at Craigflower, only the farm's old school and McKenzie's large manor house remain. Both are open for public viewing.

Roadhouses Built Miles from Fort
Six Mile Pub, Highway 1 (Island Highway) at Parson's Bridge

At one time, stage stops and inns marked the route between Victoria and Sooke. Only three—the Six Mile, Four Mile and Seventeen Mile—remain today. The mile names refer to the distance of the stage stops from Fort Victoria. Six Mile Roadhouse opened in 1855, with the present building dating from the 1920s. It was originally called Parson's Bridge Hotel because of the location of nearby Parson's Bridge, which was named for William Richard Parson. Parson operated a grist mill at the head of the harbor here. Seventeen Mile Roadhouse, 11 miles (18 km) west on the highway from here, was built in 1900 by Edward Cutler. Like Six Mile and Four Mile, Seventeen Mile Roadhouse is used today as a pub and restaurant.

Fort Rodd Hill Guards Esquimalt Harbour
Highway 1 (Island Highway), 1 mile (1.6 km) south of Six Mile Pub, Fort Rodd Hill National Historic Park, Ocean Boulevard, (just before junction with Highway 14), Colwood

Fort Rodd Hill, overlooking the entrance to Esquimalt Harbour, was built in 1895 to protect ships of the British navy that used the harbor as a West Coast headquarters. Named for the *Whyomalth,* or Esquimalt Songhee Indians, living along its shores, Esquimalt Harbour became important because its well-sheltered waters were able to accommodate vessels drawing more than 18 feet (5.5 m) of water, the upper limit for vessels trying to use Victoria's smaller harbor.

Hudson's Bay Company Chief Factor James Douglas was criticized for locating Fort Victoria on the smaller harbor, which was known then as Camosack or Camosun. Esquimalt Harbour appeared deeper, larger and better in almost every conceivable way than Victoria Harbour. Consequently, almost from the earliest days of Fort Victoria in the 1840s, Esquimalt Harbour became the more important of the two harbors and was the British headquarters for their naval operations on the Canadian West Coast. Later, the Canadian navy would do the same. Artillery batteries to guard the entrance to the harbor were first placed at Rodd Point about 20 years before the British government constructed the fort.

Fort Rodd Hill was turned over to the Canadian government by the British in 1906. When the British reduced their Pacific operations after the turn of the century, Canada took over the Esquimalt base and in 1910 established its own fleet. Four years later, with the start of World War I, German cruisers were reported in the North Pacific, and the British Columbia government bought two submarines, the *Lequique* and *Antofogasta,* from a Seattle shipyard. Later that year the provincial government turned the submarines over to the Canadian navy, and the vessels were used to patrol the west coast. Then in 1917, British Columbia lost its submarines when the navy transferred them to Halifax and the North Atlantic.

After World War II shore-based artillery became obsolete. From then on, harbors would be protected by missiles and jet aircraft. Fort Rodd Hill was outdated and closed in 1956, although the harbor at Esquimalt is still a base for Canadian naval operations on the west coast. In 1962, the fort was named a national historic site.

Dunsmuir's Son Builds His Own Castle
Royal Roads College, Highway 14, .5 miles (.8 km) south of Highway 1 (Island Highway) intersection

---

Robert Dunsmuir, founder of the Dunsmuir coal empire, built Craigdarroch Castle in Victoria. Perhaps to outdo his famous father, his son James later built an even grander castle, now part of Royal Roads College, on what was once one of the most lavish country estates in Canada. James Dunsmuir, along with his brother, Arthur, carried on the family business enterprises after his father's death. James also went into politics and became a largely ineffectual premier of British Columbia. Later, he became lieutenant governor of the province. It was while serving in this office that James Dunsmuir built his castle and developed the adjoining 700 acres (283 ha), called Hatley Estate, which overlooked the entrance to Esquimalt Harbour.

The estate's grounds featured formal Japanese and Italian gardens, horse stables and riding paths, numerous guest cottages and game courts set among a large fir forest. The 50-room castle featured the usual run of palatial dining and bedrooms found in such mansions, but it also included a large conservatory, a large ballroom and extensive library. Too expensive to maintain as a private residence after Dunsmuir's death in 1920, Hatley Estate was purchased by the federal government and turned into Royal Roads Military College. Royal Roads was taken over by the provincial government in 1996. Dunsmuir's botanical gardens have been preserved.

Pioneer Weather Stone at Sooke Still in Use
Sooke Museum, Highway 14, 29 miles (47 km) from Highway 1 (Island Highway), east side of Sooke

Probably the only weather stone still in use on Vancouver Island hangs at the gate of the Sooke Museum. A sign beside the stone explains how early settlers used these folk weather forecasting stones to understand and predict weather conditions during the days before satellite weather stations and television weather reports. According to the sign, you can easily tell the weather by observing the stone and noting the following phenomena:

1 If the stone is wet on top, it's raining.
2 If it's dry on top, then it's not raining.
3 If there is a shadow underneath, the sun is shining.
4 If the stone is white on top, it has been snowing.
5 If it swings back and forth on the chain, the wind is blowing.
6 If the stone is jumping up and down, there's an earthquake.
7 And if the stone is wet on one side, but not the top, a dog has recently passed by.

Vancouver Island Exploring Expedition Finds Gold
Highway 14, 29 miles (47 km) from Highway 1 (Island Highway), Sooke

Sooke was the jumping-off point in 1864 for Vancouver Island's only true gold rush. Ironically, the gold rush began as a result of the waning of the Cariboo Rush on the British Columbia mainland. The Fraser and then the Cariboo gold rushes had first brought Victoria into existence and then given the new community a measure of prosperity and importance. As the end of the Cariboo boom was felt, however, business concerns in Victoria began to fear tough times for the young city's economy. Everyone realized the colonies of British Columbia and Vancouver Island were likely to be joined. Citizens of Victoria also understood that unless something was done to boost Victoria's fortunes, the capital of the joined colonies could well be placed at the larger and in many ways more accommodating site of New Westminster on the mainland.

Without the seat of government and an occasional gold rush to help it along, Victoria might become a backwater. During the winter of 1863–64, a plan was hatched to stimulate local fortunes. Salvation, it was hoped, could be found in the Vancouver Island Exploring Expedition. Ostensibly, the purpose of the expedition was to explore and map the interior of Vancouver Island. But what Victorians were really after was another gold discovery—and not just any discovery, but one close enough to Victoria itself to ensure the community's continued economic well being.

Robert Brown was appointed the expedition's leader. The team included an experienced prospector named John Foley. Frederick Whymper was named the expedition's artist. Initially, the expedition worked north, following the Cowitchan River from the coast, and then crossed overland to Port San Juan. From there the party journeyed up the Sooke River, and on July 21, 1864, John Foley discovered gold on a tributary of the Sooke the men named after one of their members, Peter Leech.

With Victoria's gold strike found, the expedition loyally moved on to finish its mapping and exploration work without the services of prospector Foley, who deserted the expedition. Foley had staked claims from California to the Cariboo in almost every major North American gold rush since 1849, but he'd never made his fortune.

He was soon joined by several thousand other gold seekers. Leechtown sprang up on the river near the diggings. Miners found enough gold to spur enthusiasm, and commerce returned to Victoria. But the boom lasted for only a few months. Like so many gold rush boomtowns, the settlement on the Leech River soon faded. Gold was there all right, but not in sufficient quantity to sustain a gold rush. Men could make better wages than most laborers, but no one really got rich, including John Foley. Most of the prospectors gave up and moved on. Today, nothing remains of Leechtown except a marker placed there in the 1920s and now hidden almost completely in the tall grass.

Vancouver Island's First Settler Shoots Cow and Brings Broom to Sooke

Woodside Farm, Highway 14, 29 miles (47 km) from Highway 1 (Island Highway), Sooke

Walter Grant has been generally credited with being the first independent settler on Vancouver Island. He established a farm in the Sooke District in 1849 (at Woodside Farm at the western edge of today's town of Sooke), coming here after suffering financial difficulties in Europe. Grant began to fail here, too, almost as soon as he set foot on the island. In fact, one of his first acts after getting off the boat from Europe was to shoot a cow in today's Beacon Hill Park in downtown Victoria. Grant said that, as a greenhorn, he had mistaken the cow for a buffalo. Within a few years Grant left the island for good, but before his departure, he deposited one lasting memento in the Northwest.

During the winter of 1850, Grant spent some time in Honolulu, ostensibly to decide what to do with his future. During his Hawaiian vacation he met a Hudson's Bay Company officer who cultivated Scottish broom plants in his South Pacific garden. Grant, too, was fond of the flowers and plants of the Old World, so he brought a few broom seeds with him on his return journey to North America. The following spring he planted the seeds on his Sooke farm. Not long afterward, he got caught up in the excitement of the California Gold Rush, and, along with two of his hired men, he left the island for the gold fields. Grant was gone for two years before returning long enough to sell his farm and head for his native England. Grant never returned to Vancouver Island, but some of his broom seeds thrived and eventually spread throughout the area. Today, Scottish broom plagues most of the northwest coast. The still-spreading broom crowds out native plants and destroys pastures from British Columbia to Oregon—and Walter Grant started it all here in Sooke with a handful of seeds from Hawaii.

Muirs Mine Coal and Settle Permanently in Sooke
John Muir School at Woodside Farm, Highway 14, 29 miles (47 km) from Highway 1 (Island Highway), Sooke

When Walter Grant left Vancouver Island for England, he sold his farm to John Muir. Muir was an English miner who originally came to Vancouver Island to mine coal at Fort Rupert, a Hudson's Bay post on the island's northern coast. While Grant is usually given the title of Vancouver Island's first independent settler, in some ways Muir deserves the title more. Without any doubt, he was independent.

Muir, along with several of his relatives, was first hired to mine Hudson's Bay Company coal in 1850, the year after Walter Grant arrived on the island. A bitter dispute soon developed between the Muirs and company officers, who treated the miners in the same high-handed manner they treated all Hudson's Bay Company servants. But Muir and his relatives had no intention of being treated that way. They were, after all, miners. They said the Fort Rupert mine, with its poor-grade coal, was little better than worthless. Living conditions were intolerable. Within weeks of their arrival, the Muirs staged the first strike in what became Vancouver Island's long history of labor conflict. The company, for its part, charged several of the miners with sedition. A compromise position was eventually reached, but just as the Muirs predicted, the mines at Fort Rupert failed because of the poor quality of the coal.

The year after John Muir bought Walter Grant's farm at Sooke, the Hudson's Bay Company hired him as a foreman at a new mine opening near Nanaimo Bay. In order to maintain peace with the miners, James Douglas directed company officers to issue no orders to any miner except through Muir. Muir and his wife, Annie, continued to operate their farm and sawmill at Sooke, and many of their descendants can still be found on Vancouver Island. Although the farm, now called Woodside, is no longer owned by the Muir family, the farmhouse the Muirs built is still there, and from the outside, it looks much the way it must have when it was constructed in about 1869.

No Point to "Point No Point"
Highway 14, 15 miles (24 km) west of Sooke

Point No Point acquired its catchy name because of the confusion it caused early navigators along the Strait of Juan de Fuca. From certain places, the point of land here appeared as a promontory jutting out from the coast. From other vantage points, however, no point was visible, and there seemed to be no point in charting it. In 1895, government surveys designated the place as Glacier Point, but people continued to call it Point No Point, so the board of Canadian Geographic Place Names made that name official in 1957. A bed and breakfast operates on the site today.

Refused Drinks Almost Puts Hotel in Drink
Highway 14, 46 miles (74 km) northwest of Sooke, Port Renfrew

Historically, Port Renfrew has always been the town at the end of the road. Today, that's the West Coast Road from Victoria. Before that it was a logging railroad. The government enticed settlers into this valley at the mouth of the San Juan River in the 1880s with promises of a highway to Victoria. The promise wasn't kept until several decades later, however, and Port Renfrew existed mostly as a logging town during the intervening years.

The dockside Port Renfrew Hotel has served loggers well during much of that time. The story is still told of how a rowdy tugboat crew was once refused service and thrown out of the hotel's pub late one weekday afternoon. The disgruntled captain and crew wrapped the hotel in a towline and fired up their boat. When they began stretching the line, attempting to tow the building into the ocean, the hotel owner beat a hasty path dockside, pleading with the tugboat crew to stop. Finally, he persuaded the boatmen to leave his hotel alone by asking them inside for a beer, this time on the house.

Wreck of the *Valencia* Results in West Coast Trail
Highway 14, Port Renfrew

The southern end of the West Coast Trail lies across the bay from Port Renfrew. Today, the trail is part of Pacific Rim National Park, but it was originally called the Shipwrecked Mariners Trail or sometimes the West Coast Life Saving Trail. As the original names suggest, the trail was not built for vacationing hikers, but to rescue shipwrecked sailors marooned on the rugged and stormy west coast.

There have been many shipwrecks off the west coast of Vancouver Island, but it was the wreck of the *Valencia* in 1906 that led to the construction of the trail. The *Valencia* was an American steamer owned by the Pacific Coast Steamship Line. Under the command of Captain O.N. Johnson, she left San Francisco on January 20, 1906, on a bright sunny day, bound for Seattle with 164 passengers and crew on board. At 5:30 the following morning, after the ship passed Cape Mendocino on the Washington coast, skies clouded over, and the Captain couldn't determine his position from the stars.

Undaunted, Captain Johnson pushed on, guided by experience and instinct and seldom bothering to take depth soundings that might have accurately established the *Valencia*'s position. Forgetting to add ocean current to engine speed and unable to see in what was later described as "thick weather," the captain miscalculated the distance north he'd traveled and passed by the entrance to the Strait of Juan de Fuca. Traveling slowly, the *Valencia* finally ran aground about midnight near Pachena Point, about 15 miles (24 km) south of Cape Beale Lighthouse.

Captain Johnson immediately gave the order to reverse the engines, and the ship backed off the rocks where it had been momentarily held. But a hole had been torn in the hull, and water began to pour into the bow of the ship. Immediately, Captain Johnson called for full steam ahead, hoping to ground the ship on the rocks again rather than have it sink in open water. Outside, only the bare, hazy outline of a ridge of cliffs about 50 yards (46 m) away could be seen.

The ship seemed safe on the rocks for the moment, but nevertheless the captain had the lifeboats lowered to the deck rails. Here, panic-stricken passengers quickly pushed the crew aside and began taking to sea even though no order had been given to abandon ship. In fact, the crew's attempts to prevent the passengers from leaving only seemed to heighten their panic. All but one of the lifeboats were taken, but guided by inexperienced hands through raging seas, not one of them reached the nearby shore. Two boats, both mostly filled with women and children, capsized as they hit the water. Four others managed to stay upright in the turbulent waters near the ship but capsized before reaching shore. Most of their passengers drowned. Only a few were washed ashore alive instead of being battered against the rocks. Back on the ship, the captain calmed the remaining passengers, assuring them that the ship was safe for the time being and no attempt to reach shore should be made until morning.

But next morning, the weather was no better. The captain ordered rocket-powered harpoons shot into the distant shore. His hope was that the harpoons would lodge deeply enough in the ground to anchor ropes. The crew could then rig a boat-swain's chair to the ropes to transfer passengers from ship to shore. All but one of the harpoons failed to penetrate the rocky cliffs, however, and the rope of the successful launch broke. To make matters worse, Captain Johnson blew off two of his fingers when one of the rockets misfired.

After the last futile attempt, a Greek crew member tried to swim a rope to shore. Once in the ocean, however, he found he couldn't move against the foaming water and had to be dragged back to the ship. A passenger who had washed ashore after capsizing in one of the lifeboats tried to reach the rope of one of the spent harpoons, but the poor man was swept up in the fierce seas. Passengers on the *Valencia* watched in horror as his soon lifeless body, caught in the waves, was bashed again and again against the rocks.

As the tide rose, the *Valencia* began to settle deeper into the water. Soon the main deck was awash. Most of the passengers and crew huddled in the forward part of the saloon deck, where they were above the waves but not out of the icy spray. Many took refuge in the rigging until, without warning, the mast broke, sending people hurtling to the deck, where they were immediately washed overboard and carried to their death against the rocks.

Desperate, but still hoping to rig a boatswain's chair, the captain called for volunteers to man the last remaining lifeboat in an attempt to take a line to the cliffs. Incredibly, the boat made it to shore, but here the men discovered a telegraph line running from tree to tree along the shoreline. Under the line they found a board with the words "3 miles to Cape Beale" written as if it were a fallen road sign. Instead of continuing to the cliff to anchor the rope as they had been instructed, the men decided to proceed to Cape Beale for help. In the meantime, nine survivors from the capsized lifeboats had already followed the telegraph wires to a lineman's cabin 3 miles (5 km) south. Inside, they found a telephone and called another line shack at Clo-oose, where the lineman passed news of the wreck on to the outside world.

Rescue ships were sent from Seattle and Victoria. Volunteers started north from Clo-oose on foot and more came south from Bamfield. By the time rescue ships arrived, however, it was too dark to see, and the seas still raged under a driving rain. Wind was estimated at 20–25 miles (32–40 km) per hour. The first sailors on the scene said that on one pass near the wrecked steamer they could see 30 or 40 people clinging to the rigging. Even when light came the next morning, the rescue ships decided conditions were too risky to attempt sending a dory to the besieged ship. By this time all decks on the *Valencia* were completely submerged as the rescue ships cruised back and forth looking for survivors.

Late in the afternoon, the *City of Topeka* picked up a life raft drifting off Cape Beale with 20 people from the *Valencia*. Several were unconscious and all were near death. A few minutes later another raft was launched from the wreck and 10 more survivors were rescued. No one knew if anyone else was left alive on board. By this time only a stump of a mast and a small section of the hull were visible above water. Flotsam and jetsam littered the shore, and bodies dotted the high-water mark for miles along the coast. Many were so scoured by the rocks they were unrecognizable.

In the end, of the *Valencia's* 164 passengers and crew members, only 38 survived. Fifty-nine bodies were found. Sixty-seven people were missing and presumed drowned. The following summer, Indians from Clo-oose found a lifeboat from the wreck in a shoreline cave blocked by a large bolder. Evidently, the boat had been tossed over the rock in the storm. Eight skeletons were still in the boat when the Indians found it.

Both Canada and the United States set up commissions of inquiry to determine the cause of the sinking, how future accidents should be handled and how to prevent similar tragedies. A number of recommendations were made, including one to build a lifesaving trail on Vancouver Island's west coast between Bamfield and Port Renfrew. Work on the trail began the following spring. It was completed in 1908. From Bamfield to Shelter Bight, near where the *Valencia* sank, the trail was made 12' (3.5 m) wide so that teams of horses and wagons could be brought in with equipment to take out survivors. The trail was reduced to 4' (1.2 m) as far as Carmanah Point, where it widened again between there and Port San Juan. Sixty-two culverts and 21 bridges were built on the trail. When technology improved and modern lifesaving methods were adopted, the trail was left by default to recreational hikers. Pacific Rim National Park, of which the trail is a part, was established in 1972.

Promoters Promise to Put Clo-oose on the Map
West Coast Trail, about halfway between Bamfield and Port Renfrew

---

Gullible buyers are the land promoter's target, and in few places in North America did they find more gullibility than at Clo-oose, an isolated Indian village on the west coast of Vancouver Island. Even today there are no roads leading to the community. But at the turn of the century, real estate promoters on the Canadian prairies began selling lots here, a place they claimed would soon be a booming city larger than Victoria.

A sketch even circulated showing large wharves with waiting ships, a built-up main street complete with street cars and a beautiful sandy beach stretching into the distance. Lots were sold all over the prairies and as far away as England. Some people actually moved to their new property at Clo-oose to get an early start before the boom began. One Alberta family sold their farm to move to their West Coast property and found, once they reached Victoria, that the only way into the community was to wait for one of only three ships per month that stopped there. Once they arrived they discovered Clo-oose for what it was: a small, extremely isolated village on a wind- and rain-battered coast. The family left again on the next ship out of town, abandoning most of their possessions on the beach because shipping them back to Victoria cost more than they had left from the sale of their farm.

RETURNING TO VICTORIA AND
THE SAANICH PENINSULA

Raven Steals Baby
Highway 17, McKenzie Avenue, 4 miles (6 km) north from downtown Victoria, Saanich

North of Victoria, on the Saanich Peninsula, the oak-dotted hill to the right of Highway 17 is the setting for a Vancouver Island Christmas legend. The tale tells of a strange kidnapping that took place during the early years of Fort Victoria, probably in the winter of 1843. According to the story, a raven landed at the Indian village outside the new fort's front gate on a pleasant morning the day before Christmas. A group of people, including a newborn baby was nearby, but no one paid any attention to the raven. Before anybody could stop it, the bird picked up the infant and flew off, grasping the child or its clothing in its talons. People followed the bird on the ground as it flew away, but no one was fast enough to keep up.

Search parties looked for the baby all that day and through the long night. It wasn't until the next morning, on Christmas day, that the baby was discovered, unharmed and laughing to itself, high in a fork of a tree at the summit of this hill. Ever since, the place has been known as Christmas Hill.

Quarry Becomes Famous Garden
Keating Crossroad, Highway 17, 10.5 miles (17 km) north from downtown Victoria, Saanich

Early in the twentieth century an old quarry 4 miles (6.5 km) west of the junction of Highway 17 and Keating Crossroad at Tod Inlet was transformed into a beautiful sunken garden. The limestone quarry was owned by Robert Butchart, an early Vancouver Island businessman and cement manufacturer. Butchart's wife, Jenny, was inspired to turn the exhausted limestone quarry near their home into a place of green and growing beauty. In 1904, she hired a crew of gardeners to turn the quarry and much of the surrounding area into the world-renowned Butchart Gardens.

Tons of topsoil were brought in by horse and cart to turn the

Mill Bay, Brentwood ferry.

barren pit into a flowering sunken garden. As the years passed, other gardens were added. Many of the plants on the 35-acre (15-ha) garden, including a now huge Redwood tree brought from California in the 1930s, were collected by the Butcharts on their travels. The sunken garden features a waterfall, stream, lake and pools. Today, the grounds include a formal Japanese and Italian garden and an English rose garden where the original Butchart vegetable patch used to be. The property is still owned by Jenny Butchart's descendants.

Mt. Newton Home to First Settlers
Highway 17, 12.5 miles (20 km) north from downtown Victoria, at Mt. Newton Crossroad, Central Saanich

While Walter Grant is said to be Vancouver Island's first independent settler to buy land from the Hudson's Bay Company, the group of families who took up land near Mt. Newton on the Saanich Peninsula several years later were the first true farmers to acquire land without having to pay for it. Angus McPhail, an ex-Hudson's Bay Company employee, was probably the earliest, arriving in the area about 1855. More than half a dozen other settlers arrived by the time of the Fraser Gold Rush three years later.

With thousands of immigrants arriving during the gold rush, the company's chief factor James Douglas saw clearly that the old ways of the Hudson's Bay Company were over. No longer could he hope to completely control the economy and politics of Vancouver Island. Knowing that British Columbia's new residents would need food, and realizing he could no longer deny land to homesteaders, Douglas began in February 1859 to issue land ordinances. Initially, land was offered at 10 shillings, or 50 cents, an acre (.4 ha), but within two years it was possible to pre-empt 160 acres (65 ha) for about $25.

Strike Leads to Dogwood Fleet
Highway 17, 19.5 miles (31 km) north from downtown Victoria, Swartz Bay Ferry Terminal

---

Spirit of British Columbia, *ferry to Victoria.*

Even before British Columbia became part of Canada, privately owned shipping companies—beginning with Hudson's Bay Company ferries—carried people up and down the west coast. Vessels sailing between Victoria and the lower mainland became the crucial link that joined Vancouver Island to the rest of the province. Once the Canadian Pacific Railway reached Vancouver this link became even more important.

*Horseshoe Bay Terminal, routes to Nanaimo, Langdale and
Bowen Island.*

By the 1950s, all manner of steamship and ferry companies
operated on the British Columbia coast, but the main transportation between Victoria and the lower mainland was provided by the Canadian Pacific Steamship Company. In 1958,
employees went on strike, and service between Victoria and the
mainland halted. R.B. Bennett's Social Credit government
moved quickly to ensure that ferry service would be maintained.
It arranged to take over the operation of Black Ball Ferries, a subsidiary of the Puget Sound Navigation Company, which operated between Nanaimo and Horseshoe Bay at North Vancouver.
Under the government's plan, Black Ball was used to ensure adequate service between southern Vancouver Island and the lower
mainland. The plan might have worked, except Black Ball
employees also went on strike that July.

The day the Black Ball workers went on strike, Premier Bennett announced that the Province of British Columbia would go
into the ferry business itself. The new Pat Bay Highway (Highway
17) was nearing completion between Victoria and Sidney, so the
route was extended to Swartz Bay, then only a quiet backwater at
the tip of the Saanich Peninsula. Its main attraction was that it
was 3 miles (5 km) closer to the mainland shore than Sidney.
Bennett also announced that construction of the provincial ferry
company's first two ferries would begin immediately.

By the spring of 1960, both vessels, plus new ferry terminals at Swartz Bay and Tsawwaassen, had been built. The British Columbia Ferry Corporation, with its dogwood flower emblem flying midship from every vessel, officially began operation on June 9. The following year the government bought out Black Ball and began running ferries between Departure Bay at Nanaimo and Vancouver. In succeeding years more and more ferry routes were added until today the British Columbia Ferry Corporation runs the largest ferry service in the world, with ferries plying the entire coast from Puget Sound to the Alaska border.

Chapter 2

Island Retreats and City Streets

Swartz Bay to Tsawwassen, Vancouver and the Lower Fraser

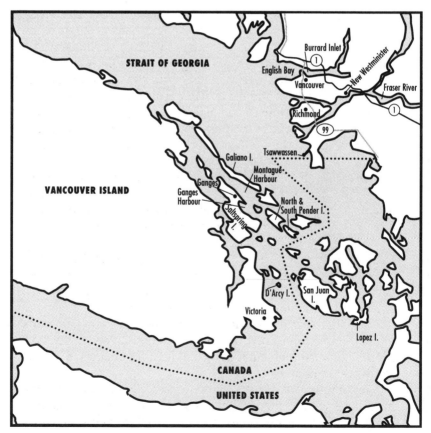

O N JUST ABOUT ANY DAY in any season, long lines of cars, trucks, vans and recreation vehicles crowd the parking lot at the Swartz Bay ferry terminal. Foot passengers push hurriedly through the terminal gates on their way to board one of the dozen or so British Columbia Ferry Corporation vessels that dock here at the northern tip of the Saanich Peninsula on south Vancouver Island. Some of the vehicles and foot passengers are bound for one or the other of the nearby Gulf Islands, but most are on their way to Vancouver, or other communities in the densely populated lower mainland, via the Tsawwassen terminal.

Today, the lower Fraser Valley is an almost uninterrupted metropolis from Vancouver to Hope, but in 1858, when the Fraser River Gold Rush began, the Fraser Valley was almost completely wild. In all of British Columbia, including southern Vancouver Island, native people accounted for almost the entire population. Two hundred nonnative people, almost all of them connected to the Hudson's Bay Company, lived huddled at the edge of the wilderness surrounding Fort Victoria. A few other whites could be found near the coal mines at Nanaimo, farther up the island at Fort Rupert or living isolated lives at scattered fur posts. On the lower Fraser, where a small post at Fort Hope and the larger Fort Langley accounted for the bulk of the mainland white population, a few prospectors scratched for gold in the gravel of the Fraser's many tributaries.

Once the gold rush burst on the scene, however, people flooded into British Columbia from all over the world. The lure of gold in the lower Fraser River Valley drew more than just prospectors. New immigrants of all sorts—traders, shopkeepers, teamsters, farmers, gamblers, prostitutes, assorted con artists, outright bandits and all manner of laboring men and women— arrived and took up residence along the Fraser and in other parts of British Columbia. The gold rush also brought the first significant settlement to southern Vancouver Island. It sparked the development of Victoria as a commercial center of more than fur trade importance. It brought the first farmers to the Gulf Islands. Other settlers built farms, homes and businesses on the southwest mainland.

For longtime residents at Fort Victoria, the new immigration must have seemed an invasion. Victoria's nonnative population jumped from a few hundred to 5,000 in a matter of weeks. Thousands of other immigrants passed through the bulging new community on their way to the Fraser and elsewhere in present-day British Columbia. Within two years prospectors were already mining in the Cariboo, where gold finds were large enough to create a second mainland gold rush by 1862. It attracted more people than the original Fraser River Gold Rush. Many of the stampeders moved on to other places after the gold petered out, but thousands stayed to make homes in the interior or along the coast of British Columbia.

On Saltspring and other Gulf Islands, where today's British Columbia Ferry Corporation vessels make regular runs, home-steaders settled down to developing British Columbia's first extensive independent farms, taking advantage of markets in the new settlements on the mainland. The little town of New Westminster, across the river from the old Hudson's Bay post at Fort Langley, became the capital of the mainland colony. By the early 1860s, Burrard Inlet's first residents began to establish themselves in the area, although it would be another genera-tion before the coming of the Canadian Pacific Railway would turn the small settlement into a new metropolis. Once the rail-road came, the new city of Vancouver almost immediately began to dominate the economy of the entire province, and by the 1990s it grew to include a metropolitan area that takes in most of the lower coast from the mainland mountains to the Gulf Islands.

De Courcy Starts Pig War Over Gulf Islands, Gains Peerage at Home
San Juan and Gulf Islands, Strait of Georgia

From their names on the map, it appears that the Gulf and San Juan islands are two separate groups that lie off the south-ern coast of Vancouver Island, near the Swartz Bay ferry terminal on the western side of the Strait of Georgia. Geographically, how-ever, the islands are actually part of one long archipelago that happens to be divided by the Canada–United States border. This political division, cutting through Haro Strait, came about after a San Juan Island farmer shot a pig, and with the help of a Victo-ria magistrate, precipitated an international incident that became known as the Pig War.

San Juan Island was the first of the islands in the archipelago to be settled. From the earliest days of Fort Victoria, the island had been used by the Hudson's Bay Company to raise hogs, sheep and cattle. Later, while Hudson's Bay Company livestock still roamed the island unmolested, San Juan's fertile soil and attractive climate lured a number of British and American homesteaders to its shores. Initially, the two nationalities got along well with each other, and only a vague American claim to the territory was made. The claim wasn't even initiated by the United States government. It was made by the Oregon legislature in 1852, when that body named all the islands off the U.S. west coast as part of its territory. No mention of Vancouver Island or any of the other British islands that lay off the American coast was made.

In 1860, Governor James Douglas appointed a magistrate in Victoria for San Juan Island. His name was Major De Courcy, a recently arrived ex-British military officer already known in Victoria for his haughty, authoritarian manner. Not long after his appointment, De Courcy ignited national tensions.

The brouhaha started when an American homesteader named Lyman Cutler shot a roaming Berkshire hog that had been rooting potatoes in his garden. The hog belonged to the Hudson's Bay Company, so De Courcy immediately prosecuted the American for the murder of the pig. Cutler was found guilty and fined about $100 for the $5 hog. He was also imprisoned. To make matters worse, De Courcy threatened other American settlers with the whole power of the British nation if they stepped out of line again. It was as if British sovereignty itself had been threatened by the killing of one hog.

American residents, quick to react after the punishment of their neighbor and De Courcy's tirade against them, appealed to General Harney, then in command of U.S. forces on Puget Sound. Without informing his superiors, Harney dispatched Captain Pickett with a small force of men from nearby Fort Bellingham. Pickett arrived on San Juan Island with instructions to lay claim to the territory in the name of the American government. When news of this measure reached Victoria, an outraged Governor James Douglas dispatched British war ships to the area in order to repel what Douglas called the American "invasion" and demanded the British government counterattack to expel the intruders.

Despite Douglas's orders the commander of the British navy in the region, Admiral Banes, refused to do anything without instructions from England. When orders finally came, they instructed Douglas to meet with American representatives to negotiate rather than fight. The British government, despite Douglas's protestations, had little interest in the Pacific Northwest and no desire to stir up trouble with the Americans over what seemed little more than a dispute over a hog. Just as the English had been willing to settle today's Canadian boundary far above the natural border of the Columbia River in order to avoid conflict, they were also willing to negotiate a lesser settlement for any of British Columbia's islands.

Arrangements were made for San Juan Island to be occupied by soldiers from both Britain and the United States until arbitration could settle the dispute. The matter took longer than anyone anticipated—over a decade—but in October 1872 the mutually agreed upon arbitrator, German Kaiser Willhelm, finally decided San Juan and other nearby islands should belong to the Americans. The Gulf Islands, the Kaiser decided, would remain Canadian.

De Courcy, who had to be rescued from Friday Harbour on San Juan in order to avoid assassination, continued his role as magistrate in Victoria after the pig affair had calmed. However, he proved almost as unpopular in Victoria as he was on San Juan. In 1861, he tired of Vancouver Island and developed a new attitude toward the Americans. With the American Civil War raging, he quit Victoria and went to Washington, D.C., where he presented his credentials to military officials and was made a colonel in the American army.

Despite distinguished service at Vicksburg and Cumberland Gap, however, De Courcy's overbearing personality again got him in trouble. This time it was with a superior officer who had him dismissed for what may have been a trumped up charge of insubordination. De Courcy left the United States for his home in Ireland. There, he found himself rather far down the list of heirs to the Kingsale peerage. But as luck would have it, one after another of the more immediate Kingsale heirs died. When Kingsale himself died, De Courcy became the Baron of Ireland.

Southernmost Gulf Island Becomes Leper Colony
D'Arcy Island Marine Park, D'Arcy Island

In the years before and after the turn of the century, many reasons were manufactured to ban Chinese immigration from British Columbia. Barring Oriental immigrants to prevent the transmission of leprosy was one of the most unfounded. Of the thousands upon thousands of Chinese immigrants to Canada, only a handful were ever discovered to have the disease. Still, fear of communicable diseases was commonly used to restrict immigration throughout the period, and in 1891, when seven cases of leprosy among Chinese immigrants were reported in the province, panic spread like a biblical plague through the white population.

A picturesque island lying about halfway between San Juan Island and Vancouver Island—an island that would one day become a marine park for wealthy boaters—offered a quick, if barbaric, political solution to the problem of leprosy. D'Arcy Island was uninhabited and of no obvious economic importance, so it was quickly turned into Canada's first and only leper colony. The handful of unfortunate victims of the disease was picked up and dumped unceremoniously on the tiny island, isolating them from the rest of the population, although leprosy is not particularly contagious. As years went by, a few more cases of leprosy were discovered in the province, and these poor souls were also removed to D'Arcy.

On D'Arcy Island no hospital was ever built; no medical assistance was ever offered. For the most part, the inhabitants of D'Arcy were left to fend for themselves. Once every three months a doctor brought supplies, which reportedly included opium. The rest of the year, D'Arcy's residents were virtual prisoners, waiting out the years for their disease to complete its inevitable course.

Massacre on Saltspring
Saltspring Island, Ganges Harbour

Today, Saltspring Island has a reputation for its quiet harbors, idyllic countryside and relaxed lifestyle. When nonnative settlers first came here, however, the island, like many of its neighbors, was often the scene of violent exchanges between Indians and settlers and also between various tribes. The Cowichan and other Coastal Salish groups of the south were particularly prone to clash with roving bands of Haida from the Queen Charlotte Islands and Kwakiutls from northern Vancouver Island or the northern British Columbia mainland. Sometimes other northern tribes, the Tsimshian and the Tlinget of southeastern Alaska would even come south to fight the local Salish.

As late as the 1860s, killings instigated by both sides in this long-standing north–south war between the native people of the coast still occurred regularly. In July 1860, a group of white settlers fishing at the north end of Saltspring Island told of one attack. According to their story two Cowichan Indians were fishing in a canoe near their boat when several war canoes belonging to northern Indians rounded the north end of the island. The Cowichans, unable to escape, sought protection by paddling quickly to the whites. Undeterred by the presence of the two white fishermen, the northerners swooped alongside and, as the white fishermen watched helplessly, pulled the Cowichans screaming from the canoe and promptly chopped off their heads. Then, taking the two heads with them as war mementos, they paddled away without harming or even threatening the whites.

A few days later, a group of nine Bella Bella men, two women and one young boy—none of whom had taken part in killing the Cowichans—made the mistake of landing their canoes at the head of Ganges Harbour, in today's town of Ganges. A large group of about 50 Cowichans happened to be camped nearby. Still suffering from the loss of their tribesmen, the Cowichan attacked the innocent Bella Bella, beheading eight of the nine men and taking the boy and two women prisoner. One of the Bella Bella escaped into the forest but was never heard from again. The whole affair was witnessed by several of Saltspring's early settlers from nearby cabin windows.

Saltspring Curse Leads to Murder
Saltspring Island

Saltspring Island's first settlers were black American immigrants who came north from California during the Fraser River

Gold Rush in 1857. Most had been born slaves on southern plantations. One of these early settlers was Howard Estes. In 1858, Estes' daughter, Sylvia, came to Saltspring with her husband, Louis Stark, and infant son, Willis. Stark had already begun a homestead on Saltspring's Broadwell Mountain. After the family unloaded their belongings from the schooner that brought them to the wilderness around Vesuvius Bay from Victoria, they watched the vessel disappear around a bend into Sansum Narrows. Before they could organize their belongings for the trek to Broadwell Mountain, a band of Bella Bella Indians appeared from the north.

As the family watched in fear, the Indians swarmed onto the beach and began harassing them. The Bella Bella volunteered to help the Starks carry their belongings but also threatened unpleasant consequences if the offer was rejected. Eventually, Louis Stark ran the Indians off at the point of his rifle. As they left, according to a Cowichan Indian accompanying the family, an angry medicine man who appeared to be leading the Bella Bella pronounced a curse of murder on Louis Stark.

Stark, who was just happy to have the Indians gone, didn't think anything more of the curse, although it was soon noticed that the Indians seemed to trouble the Stark family more than most other settlers. Often they stole produce or other items from the Stark homestead. In the 1860s, petty thievery turned to murder. William Robinson, who worked on the Stark farm, was found at his cabin, shot from behind with his throat slit with a butcher knife. No one was ever charged, but Indians remembered the curse of the Bella Bella medicine man and said Robinson had been mistaken for Stark.

The following year a similar murder was committed in the same cabin. This time the Stark's new hired man, Giles Curtis, was killed. Once more Indians in the area remembered the Bella Bella curse, but no evidence about Curtis's murderer was ever found. Concern grew so intense, however, that the government offered a $200 reward for information leading to the arrest and conviction of the killer. A young Indian woman soon came forward, accusing a Chemainus Indian of the crime. The man was arrested, tried and on the word of the woman—despite accusations of other Indians that she was a spurned and vengeful ex-lover—hanged.

Not long afterward the Stark family moved to a new homestead near Long Harbour, where they lived peacefully for 20 years. Then Louis and Sylvia, leaving Willis to look after the farm on Saltspring, moved to a new home near Nanaimo. Stark soon encountered more controversy because his new farm turned out to have rich coal deposits. For some time Stark refused offers to sell the place, and then one night he was discovered murdered. Although rumor has it that he was killed because of his intransigence, no one was ever charged in the killing. It took 30 years, but the curse of the Bella Bella medicine man had come to pass.

Sylvia Stark eventually sold out in Nanaimo and returned to the family homestead on Saltspring. Here she lived with her son Willis, who never married, until his death. Sylvia continued to live on Saltspring and became one of its most respected women. She lived until the 1940s, dying not long after her 106th birthday.

Island Divided and Joined
North and South Pender Island

Nobody's really sure anymore if Pender Island is one island or two, but there's no doubt it started out as one. In 1903, when most islanders still traveled everywhere by boat and the shortest route between Pender's east and west side was by portage over a rocky isthmus, everything changed. Islanders petitioned the government to dig a canal across the isthmus. The new channel made it easier for people to get from place to place on Pender and, only incidentally, created two islands where one had been before.

By 1950, however, roads and automobiles had long become the preferred means of transportation on the island, so the government built a bridge and tied the Penders together again. Today, whether you think of 10-square-mile (26-square-km) Pender as one island or two, there sometimes does seem to be a difference between North and South. North Pender, where most of the island's 1,500 people live, also is home to most of the businesses on the island. The ferry terminal, at Otter Bay, is on North Pender, and more homes, cottages and small acreages are evident there. South Pender retains a less settled atmosphere.

U.S. Wool Smuggler Caught with Canadian Wool
South Pender Island

From Gowlland Point on South Pender Island, there are splendid views of Boundary Pass and the American San Juan Islands. Killer whales also are occasionally spotted here, and the numerous small bays and coves offer splendid opportunities for boaters. These same coves and bays were once the common haunts of smugglers operating between Pender and the American San Juan Islands.

The Gulf and San Juan islands are really part of the same archipelago, and there has always been a good deal of social and commercial interaction between them. Although Pender's San Juan neighbors suddenly became part of another country after the international boundary was decided by Kaiser Wilhelm, the American islands were still closer than Victoria. For many years after the border was established, it was common for early settlers on Pender to shop south of the border in Friday Harbour rather than row all the way to Victoria for supplies. On the return trip Pender's settlers smuggled their goods and supplies home in the bottoms of their boats.

When prohibition came to the United States, rum-running became a lucrative occupation throughout the area. Wallace Point on the west side of Bedwell Harbour on Pender was often used as a drop-off point for liquor being loaded into American boats for the trip to ready markets across the line.

In earlier years, wool smuggling was also lucrative. One well-known thief on Pender Island was finally caught when American authorities noticed that a tiny rocky islet in the northern San Juans accounted for more raw wool sales than any other point in Washington State. Shortly afterward, the island's lone inhabitant was arrested trying to sell wool that had been secretly marked on Pender Island.

Ot-Chee-Wun Disappears Inside Mountain
Montague Harbour, Galiano Island

On the Gulf Islands in the late 1850s and early 1860s, a settler or two would occasionally disappear without a trace. Usually, these disappearances were attributed to Indian attack. Often the killings were blamed on a chief of the Lamalchi tribe called Ot-chee-wun, an Indian whose reputation had grown to mythological proportions on Vancouver Island in the eyes of white and Indian alike.

Ot-chee-wun, according to Indians living near Fort Victoria, was a hundred summers old, although he looked and fought like a man in his prime. Some claimed Ot-chee-wun could make it rain simply by raising his hand to the sky. Others said he could point at the side of a rock-faced precipice on Galiano Island and his whole band would be taken inside the mountain. Everyone said that Ot-Chee-Wun wanted to drive the white man from Indian country.

Whether or not Ot-chee-wun possessed all the powers attributed to him, there was no doubt that he built a log fortress at Lamalchi Bay on Kuper Island that was every bit the equal of the white fort at Victoria. Ot-chee-wun knew that sooner or later he would need to defend himself from the whites. And as things turned out, the day came sooner rather than later.

In April 1863, a man named Brady was killed in the Pender Islands. His partner, John Henlee, escaped and took the story of what happened to Victoria. Even before Governor Douglas had time to react to this news, another report arrived from nearby Saturna Island telling of the gruesome murder of a man and his grown daughter by Indians some time earlier. Henlee felt he would recognize some of the Indians who had been involved in Brady's murder and was dispatched with the HMS *Forward* under the command of Captain Horrace Lacelles in an attempt to track down the Indians involved. At Piers Island, Lacelles learned the identity of some of the men he was after and proceeded to Kuper Island, where they were said to be located.

At Lamalchi Bay, Lacelles sent word to Ot-chee-wun to hand over the murderers. Ot-chee-wun refused, and Lacelles began firing on the village and the log fortress at its center. In response Lamalchi warriors began firing at the ship from rifle pits at the entrance to the bay. The next day, after retreating to Cowichan Bay for the night, Lacelles returned and destroyed the Lamalchi village. Most of the Indians, however, had escaped during the night.

Three more war ships and several smaller vessels arrived from Fort Victoria that day to take up the chase. Comprised of sailors, marines and civilian volunteers, the white armada now constituted the largest military force yet assembled on the west coast, all after one Indian: Ot-chee-wun. The chief's relatives were hunted down and taken as hostages. Every rumor of Ot-chee-wun's secret location was investigated. Finally, three weeks after the search began, reports came in of unusual musket shots heard above Montague Harbour on Galiano Island.

Marines searched the area and discovered moccasin tracks leading to an opening to a small cave in the side of the mountain. It seemed an unlikely hiding place for the legendary Ot-chee-wun. Another trail led up a cliff to a stone plateau where four warriors suddenly appeared. An attempt was made to capture the men, but in the heat of gunfire the Indians disappeared as quickly as they had materialized.

For the rest of the day the plateau was searched over and over, but no trace of any Indians was found. Late in the afternoon, a small opening to a large cave was discovered hidden among some boulders and Oregon grape bushes. The whites now guessed it was the entrance to Ot-chee-wun's legendary cave. As they stood watching the opening, trying to determine a course of action, a voice spoke suddenly from what seemed to be directly beneath their feet. What, the voice demanded, were white men doing on Ot-chee-wun's island?

Ot-chee-wun was told to come out or cannons would be fired into the cave. To the surprise of everyone, Ot-chee-wun and his warriors surrendered. Three weeks later Ot-chee-wun was hanged with three others in the colonial jail yard, at present-day Bastion Square in downtown Victoria.

Name of King George Evoked Often by King George Men
Strait of Georgia

The Strait of Georgia was first explored by the Spanish, who named it *Gran Canal de Nuestra Senora del Rosario la Marinera.* The following year Captain George Vancouver arrived and, not knowing the waterway was actually a strait, renamed it the Gulf of Georgia in honor of King George.

Already English traders were touting King George as the supreme figure of authority to the natives of the Northwest. Within a short time after Vancouver's arrival, Indians began calling all English traders and sailors King George Men. Americans, on the other hand, were called Boston Men, since it seemed that almost all of them hailed from the New England trading and shipping ports near Boston.

Even after the death of King George, Hudson's Bay and colonial officials continued to invoke the dead king's name, believing it had become a firmly entrenched symbol of authority in the minds of coastal Indians. Even after the name of Vancouver's Gulf of Georgia was finally changed to the Strait of Georgia, colonial officials continued to control the native population under the authority of King George. Only in the 1860s, after white rule could never seriously be challenged again, did the mantle of authority shift to Queen Victoria.

Roberts Misses Boat
British Columbia Ferry Terminal, Tsawwassen

The prominent point of land stretching south as you approach the British Columbia ferry terminal at Tsawwassen is Point Roberts, a peninsula jutting south from Tsawwassen for 3 miles (5 km). Point Roberts was named for Captain Henry Roberts of the Royal Navy, who in 1790 commanded the HMS *Discovery* as it explored the northwest coast. George Vancouver was appointed second in command.

Before Roberts had a chance to assume command of his ship, however, difficulties with Spain over the situation at Nootka sparked the quick buildup of English ships that became known to history as the Spanish Armament. Roberts was dispatched to a Royal Navy warship, upon which he sailed to meet the Spanish fleet. When war was averted by the first Nootka Convention the British government decided it was then urgent to dispatch a ship for Nootka in order to show British presence in the area. Roberts was still away from port at the time. So the government, rather than wait for Roberts' return, quickly appointed Vancouver to take command of the *Discovery* and immediately sent the new commander to the Pacific Northwest.

In consequence, it was Vancouver rather than Roberts who became the preeminent early explorer of the British Columbia coast. Today, we have a city and island both called Vancouver instead of Roberts, but on June 12, 1792, in honor of his former commanding officer, Captain Vancouver named the point of land now in American territory south of Tsawwassen Point Roberts.

Hope Mountain People Look to Sea for Food
British Columbia Ferry Terminal, Tsawwassen

According to native legends, the Tsawwassen people living near today's ferry terminal and the town of Tsawwassen came to the area from the Hope Mountains. Winters were hard in the mountains, and Chief Tsatsen, learning of the milder winters on the coast, led his tribe down the Fraser River to the new land. Shortly after this time the wife of Tsatsen gave birth to a baby girl, Tsawwassa, or "looks to the sea."

Tsawwassa grew up to be wise and beautiful. She had many suitors, but having no desire to be burdened with children and a household, she accepted none of them. She preferred spending her time roaming the shores of the lower coast or swimming far out to sea. She became an expert hunter in the forests and could track animals as well as anyone in the tribe.

Tsawwassa was so wise that one day her father decided she should succeed him as chief of his people instead of one of his two sons. Tsawwassa cautioned against the idea, however, asking her father to hold a contest to determine the new chief. She asked her father to see which of them could gather the most food to bring back to the people. In that way, she said, the chief would be chosen by skill alone.

Tsatsen accepted Tsawwassa's advice, so she and her two brothers went off in different directions to find food. Tsawwassa's brothers had become excellent hunters when the tribe lived in the mountains, so they hunted in the forest, where their people had always found food. After many days, first one and then the other of Tsatsen's sons returned carrying meat from deer, bear, cougar, ducks, geese and salmon, as well as berries.

Unlike her brothers, Tsawwassa looked for food along the shore. Tsawwassa returned shortly after her brothers with as much meat and berries, as well as fish and baskets of shellfish. And strangest of all, but perhaps most delicious, were the wild onions she had collected along the shores of the ocean. Cooked with the other food, the onions seemed to make everything taste better. The people chose Tsawwassa as their chief at the place they called Tsawwassen because it "looked to the sea," where Tsawwassa had shown them to look for food.

Captain Vancouver Misses Fraser River
Fraser River Delta, Richmond

Captain George Vancouver charted much of the coast of British Columbia between 1792 to 1794, but somehow he missed the province's largest river. Vancouver passed by the mouth of the river in June of 1792. Although he was already using row boats to explore sections of the coast where the larger sailing ships could not safely travel, Vancouver failed to note the significance of the area where the Fraser enters the sea. He wrote that the area between Point Roberts and Point Grey was "very low land, apparently a swampy flat, that retires several miles before the country rises to meet the rugged snowy mountains, which we found still continuing in a direction nearly along the coast."

Vancouver did note that there were two openings into the lowlands that he thought suitable for canoe travel. Had he explored the area during high water, he could have traveled closer to the shoreline and would undoubtedly have found the Fraser River. Instead, after his examination of this coastline, he retreated across the Strait of Georgia to anchor for the night near Galiano Island. The next day he resumed his exploration of the mainland coast farther north. Meanwhile, the Spanish also explored the region, but stayed too far out to sea to discover the river.

Vancouver continued exploring the northwest coast, with the Spanish in 1792 and on his own for the following two summers, until he finally completed his work near the present town of Petersburg, Alaska, in August, 1794. By the time his ship, the *Discovery*, returned to England it had traveled more than 65,000 miles (104,606 km). His rowboats had added another 10,000 miles (16,093 km) to that total while exploring the inner coast. And for more than 50 years afterward, Vancouver's charts would be the best maps available of the northwest coast—even though the Fraser River had been passed over. Putting the course of the Fraser on the map would be left for Simon Fraser after he followed the river from the interior in 1808.

Fraser Runs Hell's Gate, Discovers River
Highway 99, Fraser River

While Captain George Vancouver, the Spanish and others explored the south coast by sea, it would be left to fur trader Simon Fraser to discover the river that now bears his name. Fraser came to the river in 1805 from the interior after crossing the northern Rocky Mountains as an employee of the North West Company. In the spring of 1808, Fraser led an expedition down the interior river that would one day be named after him, but at that time was thought to be the upper reaches of the Columbia River.

Fraser, John Stuart, John Quesnel, nineteen voyageurs and two Indian guides set out in May from the Cariboo region in four canoes, two of which were named *Determination* and *Perseverance*. Unknown to Fraser, the high waters of spring made May the most dangerous time of year to travel on an always treacherous river. As they traveled south, Fraser found himself on a raging torrent in full spring runoff. The farther south they traveled, the worse their situation became. By June, rapids too dangerous to paddle were forcing the expedition into long portages. On June 6, a Shuswap chief was hired as a guide, even though the man insisted the river downstream was so dangerous that Fraser would never safely get through.

Fraser ignored the warning, intent on following the great river to its mouth. It was obvious by this time that the river would never lead to the Columbia, and as the journey continued even Fraser's spirit began to flag. On June 12, Indians told them that although the ocean was only 10 days away they shouldn't continue. The river, they said, was too wild; even Indians would not travel on it. Finally, Fraser had to admit the journey could not be made entirely by water. The canoes were abandoned, and the men set out on foot to follow the river to its destination on the Pacific.

Even on foot, Fraser would never have found his way without the aid of the Indians he met. At Hell's Gate, the trail almost disappeared. Only the Indians could find the mere traces of a path scattered through the rocks. "We had to pass where no human should ever venture," Fraser wrote. Sometimes, the men crossed bridges made of single poles laid between cliff-side walls. Fraser said these bridges "furnished safe and convenient passage to the natives—but we, who had not the advantages of their experience, were often in imminent danger."

After the canyon, the river became navigable once more, but the Indians became more dangerous. The first native group Fraser encountered only reluctantly agreed to rent the expedition canoes, and they warned the party that the Cowichans they would meet at the mouth of the river were bloodthirsty killers. Still, even though Fraser knew his river was not the Columbia, he insisted on following it to the sea. When he reached Musqueam at the mouth of the Fraser, he found the warnings about the coastal tribes apparently worth heeding. Fraser later wrote that as they descended the river they saw Indians coming from every direction "howling like wolves and brandishing war clubs." Close enough to the ocean to be able to see it in the distance, Fraser's party abandoned their journey of discovery and fled back to the canyon, where they prepared for their return trip upstream.

Indian Trader Starts Gold Rush
Highway 99, Fraser River

Occasional prospectors made their way as far north as the Fraser River in the early 1850s, but the mineral wealth of the river and its tributaries lay largely unexplored until the gold rush of 1858. Prospectors working north from Washington and Idaho had penetrated the Fraser River Country as far as the Thompson by 1857, but ironically the gold rush didn't begin with any of their discoveries. It began when a trader named Macaulay got arrested for trading whiskey to Indians.

In November 1857 the HMS *Plumper,* a British survey ship, along with the American survey ship *Active* were fixing the position of the Canada–United States boundary at Semiahmoo Bay. While visiting surveying camps on shore, officers of the *Plumper* caught Macaulay with a shipment of liquor for the Indians. Since the two surveying ships had been working in consort, Macauley was sent to Esquimalt on board the American vessel. On route, Macauley showed members of the crew a large quantity of gold dust traded to him by Fraser River Indians.

After delivering Macaulay to the naval base at Esquimalt, and with its work finished along the border, the *Active* returned

Active Pass, ferry to Victoria.

to its home port of San Francisco. Crew members brought news of Fraser River gold home with them to California, and the following spring Victoria received the first of the thousands of gold seekers hurrying to the new diggings along the Fraser River. More prospectors arrived on that first ship than there were residents of Victoria at the time. Within a matter of weeks, new settlements were springing up all along the Fraser River.

Queen Makes Queenborough New Westminster
Highway 1, New Westminster

After the gold rush began in 1858, British Columbia became a colony on its own, distinct from the Colony of Vancouver Island and its capital in Victoria. Although James Douglas was governor of both colonies, for a time the mainland colony was seen as a separate entity and given a capital of its own.

At first Douglas planned to build the new capital on level ground near the long-established Fort Langley on the south side of the river in the lower Fraser Valley. But Colonel Richard Clement Moody, commander of a detachment of Royal Engineers and lieutenant governor of the new colony, had other ideas. When he arrived from England in December 1858, Moody decided Douglas's town site was militarily unsuitable. Moody determined to build the capital on the north side of the river, where it would be easier to defend from American attack.

Despite the fact that Douglas had already begun selling lots at Fort Langley, a new capital was laid out on the north side of the river and the sale of more lots commenced. Trouble and confusion over the new town continued after residents of Victoria, particularly that young city's merchants, became angered at the new capital's proposed name of Queenborough. It, said the Victorians, was too much like the name of their own fair city which, after all, was the true and original Queen City. The colonial secretary, William A.G. Young, tried to appease Victorian civic pride. He declared that the name of the mainland capital would no longer be Queenborough, which could only mean Queen Victoria's city. Instead, Young declared the new capital to be known as Queensborough, or City of Queens, which would make it quite different than the Queen City of Victoria.

Citizens of Victoria, however, were not satisfied. Soon, they made such a clatter about it that the British government went to Queen Victoria and asked her to chose a different name for the new capital in far-off British Columbia. The Queen gave the matter due consideration and promptly proclaimed the place New Westminster on July 20, 1859.

Capital of Combined Colony Moved to Victoria
Highway 1, New Westminster

New Westminster served as the capital of British Columbia from 1859 until 1866. That's when it became the capital of both mainland British Columbia and Vancouver Island. After the two colonies were united by the British government in November, the seat of government on the British West Coast moved to the mainland. Then, in 1868, the legislative council of the united colonies voted fourteen to five to move the capital to Victoria. The five mainland representatives voted against the move, of course, but the matter carried because the council was controlled by imperially appointed government officials who, along with Victoria's elected representatives, preferred the comforts of Victoria to the relatively rough frontier settlement of New Westminster.

Cowboy Jack Terry and Others Smuggle Chinese
Fraser River, New Westminster

Smuggling can be a lucrative occupation along any deserted sea coast near an international boundary, and the waters off British Columbia and Washington State in the late nineteenth and early twentieth centuries were no exception. One of the most horrid instances of smuggling took place here for several years beginning in the 1880s.

At that time there were many Chinese in British Columbia who had worked on the Canadian Pacific Railway but who had been left jobless after the railroad was completed. Many of these men settled down and started businesses and farms in British Columbia. Others moved on to San Francisco, most of them illegally.

The standard rate for smuggling Chinese immigrants into the United States was $50. One New Westminster smuggler would load his boat with Chinese here and drop them off in a secluded bay near Bellingham, Washington. Before leaving New Westminster, each Chinese immigrant, in addition to paying his $50, had to agree to be sewn into a weighted burlap bag. If the boat was approached by American customs officers, the bags were quickly thrown overboard. Nobody knows how many times the smuggler saved himself by emptying his struggling cargo into the sea.

A smuggler active out of New Westminster during this time was Cowboy Jack Terry. Terry smuggled Chinese immigrants along an overland route over the old Hudson's Bay Company trails between Fort Langley and Ferndale, Washington. When the Bellingham and British Columbia Railroad was completed to Sumas in 1891, Terry decided to try a new method for taking his charges south. Instead of following trails through the giant forests, one night he stole a railroad hand car and got his Chinese customers to propel themselves down the track toward Bellingham. At Sedro Wolley, however, Terry ran into an American Customs patrol. When ordered to stop, Terry started shooting. One American officer was killed, the Chinese slipped into the forest, and Cowboy Jack, badly wounded, retreated up the track and back across the border. The experience soured him on smuggling human beings, and he apparently never entered the trade again. He did, however, continue to smuggle smaller items like diamonds and opium for many years thereafter.

Spanish Explore British Columbia Coast with Captain Vancouver

Strait of Georgia at Burrard Inlet, Spanish Banks, Vancouver

Sir Francis Drake discovered the straits of Juan de Fuca and Georgia in 1579, but in the following 200 years both straits lay forgotten and unexplored by Europeans. Finally, in 1787, British Captain Charles Barkley rediscovered Juan de Fuca Strait. Three years later several Spanish ships entered the strait far enough to explore the Gulf Islands, the open waters of the Strait of Georgia, and the shores of today's British Columbia mainland. Other Spanish ships returned the following year, including the *Santa Saturnina*, captained by Jose Maria Narvaez, who became the first to explore the coast of British Columbia as far north as today's city of Vancouver.

The *Santa Saturnina*, like other Spanish ships exploring the Northwest, was a remarkably small vessel, only 37' (11 m) long with a crew of perhaps as few as 15 men. Narvaez explored Haro and Rosario straits in today's San Juan Islands and visited Nanaimo Harbour and several of the Gulf Islands. He also explored the area off today's Point Roberts, near where the 49th parallel marks today's Canada–United States border.

The next year Spanish exploration of the Strait of Georgia continued with crews from two larger ships, the 50' (15-m) *Sutil* and the *Mexicana*, mapping the coast north from near the present international boundary. Captain George Vancouver, commanding the *Chatham* and the *Discovery*, also was exploring the Strait of Georgia at this time. Vancouver, who had sailed in the region 14 years earlier with Captain Cook, named the strait, which he still called a gulf, after King George III.

The two nations met near Boundary Bay, when the *Chatham*, commanded by Lieutenant William Broughton, encountered the *Sutil* and *Mexicana* on June 13, 1792. Broughton brought his ship alongside the *Sutil* and asked permission to come aboard, which the Spanish Captain Galiano granted. Broughton offered Galiano greetings from Vancouver and an offer of assistance. The Spanish officer extended the same courtesies to Broughton in return, in the name of Captain Francisco de Bogeta y Quadra, Spain's commanding officer in the region.

Meanwhile, that same day, Vancouver sailed into Burrard Inlet, where the city of Vancouver stands today. Vancouver took no particular notice of the area that would one day take his name, other than to note that the peninsula where Stanley Park is today was an island—which it may have been at that time.

A few days later, near today's Point Grey, just south of the Spanish Banks, Vancouver also encountered the two Spanish vessels. Both captains shared information, although the Spanish had the most to share at the time. In the days to come, however, Vancouver worked with the Spanish explorers, and together they managed to gather a great deal of information about the British Columbia coast. They concluded that the water they were exploring was a strait instead of a gulf and that Vancouver Island was indeed an island and not part of the mainland as Vancouver had previously assumed. Indeed, the name chosen for the large island, Vancouver and Quadra's Island, was to honor the two commanding officers who became close friends during their time in the Northwest. Eventually, however, Quadra's name was dropped from official maps, although it reappears on today's maps as one of the northern Gulf Islands. Vancouver also named other places along the coast with Spanish names and words to honor Spain's presence in the Northwest. Prominent among these is the name Spanish Banks on today's Vancouver shore.

Three Greenhorns First to Settle Vancouver
Highway 99, Stanley Park, downtown Vancouver

The first settlers in what became the city of Vancouver were three Englishmen known universally in the 1860s as "the three greenhorns." And greenhorns they were. John Morton, William Hailstone and Sam Brighouse had come from England in 1862 to join the Cariboo Gold Rush. Riches eluded the trio in the Cariboo. But back in New Westminster that summer, Morton stopped to look in a store window at a piece of coal on display there.

Morton had been a potter in England and knew that clay was often found in the same vicinity as coal. He inquired and learned the coal in the window had come from the south shore of Burrard Inlet. The next morning the young Englishman arranged for an Indian guide and headed for the forested shores that would, in 25 years, be part of a new Canadian city. Morton found plenty of coal, but very little in the way of clay. Still, something about the area attracted him, and back in New Westminster he convinced his two friends to form a partnership and stake a claim for land there.

With a little investigation the three greenhorns found that the land we know today as downtown Vancouver was neither surveyed nor staked. The local magistrate, Charles Brew, assured the three that if they staked and lived on property on Burrard Inlet, they would be recognized as owners once the region was surveyed. They immediately staked about 550 acres (223 ha), running from Burrard Inlet to False Creek, bordering what is now Stanley Park in Vancouver's West End. Of the three, it was Morton who spent the most time on the claim. When other settlers began arriving in the area, he already was tending a few cows. He also made bricks for a time.

Eventually, the three greenhorns subdivided their land. Morton and Brighouse merged their two-thirds and in 1882 tried to start a town they called Liverpool. But by then the Canadian Pacific Railway was already moving west, and the birth of the City of Vancouver was only four years away. Their land, which originally cost them $1 per acre (.4 ha), would skyrocket in value. By the time the first passenger train arrived in Vancouver, an estimate at the time had the three greenhorns owning property worth more than $250,000.

Beaver Washed Aground with Drunken Crew
Highway 99, Stanley Park, downtown Vancouver

For more than 50 years the Hudson's Bay Company's paddle steamship *Beaver* was the most famous vessel on the northwest coast. The 101' (31-m) *Beaver* was built in London and launched in the spring of 1835 as a sailing vessel, without being outfitted for steam. Later that summer the *Beaver* left under sail for the horn of South America. Stopping at Honolulu for the winter, the vessel then sailed for the Northwest and arrived at the mouth of the Columbia River in March 1836. By early April the craft had made its way past the treacherous sandbars at the river mouth to anchor off Fort Vancouver. It was here that the work began assembling the craft's engines, boilers and paddles to turn the sailing vessel into the Northwest's first steamship.

Once fitted for steam the *Beaver* made its way out of the river

The wreck of the SS Beaver, the first steamboat on the British Columbia coast, 1889. It was left to rot off the beaches of Stanley Park.

into the Pacific. During the next 50 years of service to the Hudson's Bay Company and others, the *Beaver* would never again enter the Columbia River. It would, however, travel almost everywhere else on the north Pacific coast, from Oregon to southeastern Alaska. For more than 20 years the *Beaver* would remain the only steam vessel in the region. Beginning in 1863, she was employed by the British navy, under the command of Daniel Pender, to survey the British Columbia coastline.

In 1870, she was returned to the service of the Hudson's Bay Company. In 1874, the company sold the ship to Stafford, Sanders, Morton, and Company of Victoria, which used her as a general freight vessel and towboat along the coast. Then, in July 1888, at Prospect Point at the entrance of Vancouver Harbour, the *Beaver*'s captain and crew, after a night of heavy drinking, allowed the historic craft to be carried by the tidal current into the rocks, where the old steamer ignobly ended 52 years of service on the northwest coast. Several British Columbia landmarks, including Beaver Harbour, Beaver Cove, Beaver Island, Beaver Creek and at least two Beaver Rocks are named after the historic steam paddler.

The Hudson's Bay Company's Sea Otter *was the second steamship on the British Columbia coast. It is shown here at Bella Coola.*

Gassy Jack Robbed in Gastown
Intersection of Carrall and Water streets, Gastown, Vancouver

The first store in downtown Vancouver is often credited to "Gassy" Jack Deighton. Deighton arrived in 1867 on the bank of Burrard Inlet, near the Hastings sawmill, with a barrel of whiskey, a yellow dog, a few chairs, a pair of chickens, his wife and a couple of her Indian relatives. A former Fraser River steamboat man, Deighton invited men from the mill to have a glass or two of whiskey with him as they passed by his boat. While they drank he explained that, though lacking funds, he was about to start a business and could use their help constructing a building. Inside of 24 hours the whiskey was gone, but a log building Deighton called the Globe Hotel stood amongst the trees.

Deighton's new saloon became the center of social life in the little frontier town that would one day be known as Vancouver. Deighton was a garrulous sort, and people jokingly nicknamed him Gassy Jack because of his constant chatter. As time went on and others built cabins or businesses nearby, the entire area began to be known as Gassy Jack's town, or simply Gastown. In 1870, a surveyor determined that the Globe Hotel was in the middle of the proposed intersection of Carrall and Water Streets, so Deighton moved his building to a lot nearby, enlarged the premises and called it by the new name of Deighton House. Like his earlier saloon, Deighton House became the soul of the growing community and remained so until Jack returned to the steamboat business on the Fraser River in 1874. He died the following year.

In the early days, though, before Gassy Jack enlarged the Globe, he used to keep his money in a cigar box behind the bar. At night Jack locked the cigar box, which he called his safe, in the drawer of a nearby cabinet. No other protection was deemed necessary. Jack was a trusting fellow, and besides he knew almost everyone who came to his saloon.

But early one evening, an older man and a young woman arrived on horseback at Gassy Jack's. They were, the older man said, father and daughter and Jack took an immediate liking to the daughter, whose quiet, shy manner only added to her beauty. At supper the regular patrons of the establishment enjoyed more elaborate fare than the baked beans and pork that was generally served at Gassy Jack's. Afterward, the young woman entertained briefly by playing a couple of songs on the piano and then retired to her room. Before she left she let it be known that she wished her father would go to bed soon, implying that he might have a problem staying away from the saloon's liquor.

The father, however, obviously enjoyed the company of Gassy Jack and the other patrons and was soon buying drinks for the house. Everyone stayed up well past midnight trading rounds and generally having a high old time. The next morning, though, when Jack came downstairs, he was greeted by his stableman, who also had just woken up. The horses belonging to the inn's two visitors, he said, had been stolen. Jack immediately went upstairs to wake his guests and tell them the news. No one answered when he knocked on the father's door, however, so he opened the door only to find an empty room. He tried knocking at the daughter's door, but again there was no answer. He peeked into the room and saw her shiny black hair above the covers at the top of the bed. He quickly pulled the door closed.

Jack and his staff decided the young woman had to be told about her missing father and horses, so Jack knocked at the door again. No answer. He knocked louder. Still there was no answer. Finally, deciding the young woman had to be wakened, he opened the door and called to her. When he heard no response, Jack walked in to tap her on the shoulder. But all there was in the bed was a wig.

Finally, Jack began to realize what had happened. He turned and ran back downstairs, where he found that the drawer with his cigar box "safe" had been pried open. His money, about $400, was missing. A posse was soon assembled, and the angry men rode for New Westminster. Here they learned that two men had ridden through early that morning, apparently bound for the American border, where British law couldn't follow. Later, it was discovered that the two men were from an American theater company. They had learned of Jack's easy ways with his money and had traveled north in disguise to get it. A warrant was issued, but no one was ever arrested. Jack returned to Gastown, where he bought a metal safe and kept a closer eye on his cash.

Sudden Jerk Early Tug on Burrard
Burrard Inlet, Vancouver

Perhaps the first steam-powered boat to operate exclusively on Burrard Inlet was the *Union*. The little steamer was a home-made affair made from a threshing machine steam engine and a small, square-ended scow fitted with a pair of paddle wheels on each side. Despite her small size, the *Union* went into the towing business and made out all right for a few years before other, more suitably powered tugs took over the business.

Since the *Union* lacked the necessary power to work from a standing start, her normal course of operation was to begin any job by letting out enough slack line to give herself a good run at it. The diminutive vessel would chug away at full speed until the rope tightened with a sudden jerk and its tow lurched forward, dragging the poor *Union* nearly to a stop. Nevertheless, under full steam, and with the forward momentum provided by the initial pull, she was usually able to complete her haul, inching loads up or down the inlet once she got underway. Almost immediately after going into business, however, the *Union* became known to everyone on the inlet as the *Sudden Jerk* because of her unique starts.

Van Horne Names and Creates Vancouver
Burrard Inlet, Vancouver

When Canadian Pacific Railway officials first decided to build the transcontinental railroad west across the southern edge of the country, the head of Burrard Inlet at today's Port Moody was selected as the end of steel. The railroad's western terminus, of course, was certain to become a major city, and the new settlement of Port Moody grew in anticipation of the great future fated for it.

All across the country, however, towns were being made or destroyed by the whims of the railroad. Towns were created where the CPR built stations. Other settlements that already existed were abandoned when the railroad passed them by. The CPR's general manager, William Cornelius Van Horne, could wipe out a community's prospects with the stroke of a pencil. At Port Moody, things were to be no different. Excitement increased as construction of the railroad began. The local newspaper, the *Gazette*, predicted that buildings, paved streets, theaters, churches and industry of all sorts would soon appear as if by magic. The price of lots in the town soon increased to $2,000 and more.

But William Van Horne had ideas of his own. The railroad, he knew, would need level ground, and Port Moody had comparatively little of it. Farther west, near the mouth of the inlet at Granville (popularly called Gastown), prospects looked better. There also was the advantage of obtaining more land from the province by extending the railroad. The province, of course, would have an easier time selling the land on Burrard Inlet if the railroad were there, so provincial officials also saw the benefit of extending the line. Van Horne let it be known that although Port Moody had been selected as the western terminus he was willing to move farther west to the mouth of the inlet if suitable land grants and additional subsidies were given to the CPR. In truth, Van Horne and the CPR planned to extend the line with or without subsidies, but the CPR was always quick to negotiate better arrangements and additional government money whenever it could.

Van Horne convinced government officials that he had to have concessions or the railroad would end at Port Moody. The province quickly gave the railroad 6,000 acres (2,428 ha) of additional land along the waterfront at Burrard Inlet, land that would one day become the most valuable in Vancouver. But Van Horne also managed to extract a promise for additional concessions and the guarantee of even more land in subsequent years. Needless to say, the railroad accepted the province's offer and the railroad continued west from Port Moody.

The only problem left was a name for the future city at the new end of the line. Neither Granville, Gastown or even nearby Hastings were fitting names so far as Van Horne was concerned. This, after all, would be the western terminus of his railroad and, perhaps, the greatest city in the Canadian West. To Van Horne, Vancouver, the name of the great explorer of the Northwest, seemed more fitting. Besides, he liked the fact that the new city would start with a "Van," like his own name. Although local residents objected, government officials in Victoria accepted Van Horne's suggestion to name the new city Vancouver.

Vancouver Island residents also objected because the additional use of Vancouver's name would lead to confusion between the new city and Vancouver Island. The *Victoria Colonist,* which later became the *Victoria Times-Colonist,* suggested that since Vancouver Island had originally been named Vancouver and Quadra's Island, the new city should be called Quadra. In the provincial legislature one member decried the fact that an American citizen, Van Horne, would name a new Canadian city over the objections of so many residents. Other members of the legislature voiced similar criticisms, but in the end the government sided with Van Horne, and in April 1886, it incorporated the new city at the western terminus of the railroad under the name Vancouver.

To the dismay of the residents of Port Moody, Van Horne took his railroad past them to the new settlement on Burrard Inlet. And just as expected, British Columbia's largest city grew where the railroad ended. Port Moody, in contrast, was destined to become a distant suburb. Today, many residents prefer it that way.

Fire Burns City
Downtown Vancouver

June 13, 1886, was a sunny pleasant Sunday in the new city of Vancouver, incorporated scarcely two months before. Most of the construction work had stopped for the day, but all around was evidence of a city taking shape. New shops, hotels, homes

Hudson's Bay Company Vancouver store, Cordova Street (1887–93).

and office buildings had already spread from Burrard Inlet to False Creek. Unfinished buildings were almost as numerous as the completed ones, and only a few of these were much more than a year old. South and west of the main settlement, slag piles burned where the Canadian Pacific Railway was clearing land for its new railroad yards. Smoke from these fires, along with that from smaller clearing projects, drifted over and through the young town's newly marked streets.

No one knows which fire led to the burning of the city. But there's no doubt the flames came from the southwest, where a wind from that direction sprang to life in the early afternoon and blew sparks from the slag piles toward the boomtown taking shape nearby. Contemporary accounts all agree about the speed with which the fire spread. Perhaps because so much of the recent construction was done with freshly cut lumber, with the undried pitch still oozing from the wood, the young city seemed almost to explode in flame. Fires spread along wooden sidewalks faster than people could run. Men, women and children had to flee down the middle of roads in order to avoid the flames that soon passed them on the sidewalks. Buildings didn't seem to catch fire and burn. As flames from the spreading fire approached them, they just got hot and burst into flame, with the fire seeming to consume the entire structure in one explosive gulp.

Everything happened so fast that few people who survived

had time to save anything but themselves. The only safety seemed to be in the water itself or in areas where clearings provided protection against the flames. At least one woman and her child tried to find safety in a well, but the flames sucked the oxygen out and both suffocated. So fast did the fire spread that a man fleeing with horse and wagon down Water Street was caught from behind by the flames and both horse and driver burned. One man reported that as he fled to the water he stopped long enough to grab a child at one house and call to the mother to follow. She lingered, looking for a pair of boots, and the house burst into flame.

The city's destruction was almost complete. Only a half-dozen houses on the fringes of the town remained after the fire had run its course. The Regina Hotel on Water Street survived, saved only because of a small clearing around it and the furious efforts of men and women who found themselves stranded there by the fire. Their only hope of survival had been to douse the flames that repeatedly burst to life all around the building as the city burned around them. Miraculously, most of the city's 3,000 or so residents also survived. No one knows how many perished, because no one knows the population of Vancouver when the fire started. About 20 bodies were recovered, but perhaps twice that many died.

Within hours of the fire, the rebuilding of Vancouver had begun. By 3:00 A.M. the next morning lumber wagons were already rolling in from the Fraser Valley. By daylight framed buildings stood where nothing but hot ashes had been the night before. Within three days Water Street boasted a three-story hotel and a couple of new stores. Carrall Street had several stores, a saloon, a real-estate office and a hotel. In less than a year the first passenger train arrived in Vancouver from the east.

Joe Fortes Becomes Lifeguard
Joe Fortes Memorial, English Bay, Vancouver

A memorial plaque on a drinking fountain here commemorates the life of Joe Fortes, one of Vancouver's most popular citizens in the years before and after the turn of the twentieth century. Fortes was born in the Caribbean, became a sailor and then spent a number of years in Liverpool, England. He came to the coast in 1885 as a sailor on the ship *Robert Kerr.* Fortes must have liked what he saw in Vancouver. He chucked the sailor's life, became a Canadian immigrant and went to work in a Vancouver sawmill. During the great Vancouver fire he was reportedly responsible for saving the lives of a woman and child. Later, he worked at one of the city's hotels as a bartender.

But Fortes spent most of his free time at the beach at English Bay. He swam every day of the year, winter and summer, and appointed himself the unofficial custodian of the beach, assuming the duties of lifeguard and swimming instructor for the city's children. In 1900, the city made Fortes's position official, appointing him a special constable. A cottage was moved to the beach for Fortes to live in, and it immediately became one of the most popular spots in town as visitors came and went until Fortes's death in 1922. In addition to the memorial at English Bay, a nearby library branch and restaurant also bear Fortes's name.

Tall Tree or Tall Tale
Lynn Valley, North Vancouver

For at least 50 years there have been stories about a huge British Columbia fir tree—as tall as a skyscraper and as big around as a small house—that was said to be the largest tree ever cut in North America. The story holds that the tree was cut in the Lynn Valley in the 1890s. In 1946, the *Vancouver Sun* even printed a photograph, said to be the felled tree, with several men perched on its horizontal trunk a good 20' (6 m) above the ground.

According to the *Sun's* accompanying story, the huge Douglas fir measured 77' (23 m) in circumference, with a diameter of 25' (7.5 m) and a height of 417' (127 m). At 200' (61 m), according to the story, the tree's diameter was still 9' (2.7 m) and the first branch appeared at 300' (91 m). Although this is nearly twice the size of any other Douglas fir ever cut in the lower mainland, stories of the huge tree persist, often citing the *Sun* photograph as proof.

Many historians, however, doubt if the tree ever existed. There is no historical documentation to corroborate the photograph and no mention of the tree in early histories of the area. Besides, say the skeptics, loggers in the 1890s would never have cut a tree of such proportions. Sawmills of that time would not have been capable of dealing with it. Saw blades would not have

Logging in early Vancouver.

been big enough. Other handling tools would have been inadequate. Several foresters who have examined the photograph also claim the photograph is a hoax. The tree in the picture, they say, appears to be a Redwood, probably from California, and not a Douglas fir. Still, the story persists.

Cattle Die on Burrard Inlet Cattle Trail
Lynn Valley Road, North Vancouver

In the early 1870s, ranchers and sawmill operators from the interior began lobbying the government to build a cattle trail from Lillooet to Burrard Inlet. This would give the ranchers a market for their cattle and provide a source of fresh meat for the sawmill workers. At first the government resisted the notion, but finally enough pressure was brought to bear that construction began in the spring of 1873.

By any measure it was an ill-considered decision. At least half a dozen contractors worked on the trail over the next five years, but it took A.J. McLellan, who built the wagon road between Surrey and Langley in 1875, to finally finish it. The portion of the trail from Squamish to today's North Vancouver was the most difficult section, and McLellan, after surveying the route, recommended that the road end at the head of Howe

Ferry to Nanaimo and Langdale.

Sound and that the idea of building a road to Burrard Inlet be abandoned. But the government had committed itself to a Burrard Inlet road, so McLellan was ordered to proceed.

From Squamish, McLellan built a road that varied in width from between 3' (.9 m) and 5' (1.5 m). It traveled along the Mamquam River, over a steep mountain pass to Indian River and then through another pass to the headwaters of Lynn Creek, which it followed downstream to Burrard Inlet. Finally, after five years, about 100 bridges and $40,000 the Lilloet to Burrard Cattle Trail was completed in 1877. The first herd to use the trail headed for salt water that fall.

Two ranchers and an Indian cowboy started out from Lilloet with 200 head of fattened steers. It was already late in the season in the high plateaus, however, and little in the way of feed was found along the 135-mile (217-km) trail. Many of the bridges had already been washed away, and whole sections of the road were so steep that the cattle balked at the climb. Soon, with many animals too weak to be forced on, the drovers began to abandon cattle on the trail. Somewhere between Squamish and North Vancouver, the three cowboys gave up, turning their few remaining steers back toward the interior. No other rancher ever attempted to bring cattle over the same route. The Lilloet and Burrard Cattle Trail was abandoned without a single cow being driven over the mountains to North Vancouver.

Chapter 3

The Big Island

Victoria to Cape Scott

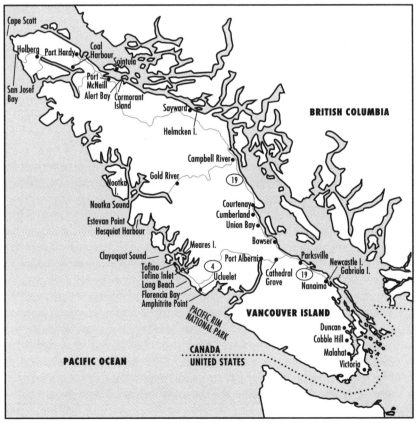

TWENTY MILES (32 km) up Highway 1 (the Island Highway) from downtown Victoria, travelers cross the Malahat Ridge to leave Victoria and the southern end of Vancouver Island behind. From a highway viewing point at the top of the Malahat, 1,156' (352 km) above the sea below, you can usually see sailboats and sometimes huge freighters bound for the open ocean beyond the Strait of Juan de Fuca. There are spectacular views of the Gulf Islands, the San Juans, the Saanich Peninsula across the inlet and the snow-covered peak of Mt. Baker across the Strait of Georgia on the North American mainland. Ahead, along the jagged shores of Vancouver Island, the Island Highway leads to Mill Bay, Cobble Hill, Duncan, and all the coastal towns to the north.

It's barely 300 miles (483 km) up-island from the Malahat summit to Port Hardy, but the towns and countryside along the way display surprising diversity. In the more populated south, traffic is thicker and the towns closer together. As you approach the Cowichan Valley, dairy farms and grazing cattle sprinkle the landscape between suburban homes, golf courses, tourist shops, and forests. At Nanaimo, with its harbor and historic downtown, Highway 19 leads north through the mid-island communities of Parksville, Qualicum Beach, Courtenay and Comox. After Campbell River, the highway abandons the shoreline for a while and becomes a northern road stretching northwest of fir and cedar forests to Port McNeil and then Port Hardy near the northern tip

Queen of Alberni, *Tsawwassen–Nanaimo route.*

of Vancouver Island. Just south of Port Hardy, at the British Columbia Ferry terminal, today's travelers can board a ferry to cross the Queen Charlotte Strait, travel the rest of the way up the British Columbia coast, along the Inside Passage and all the way to Prince Rupert near the Alaskan border.

Malahat Ridge Blasted for Road
Malahat Summit, Highway 1, 14 miles (22.5 km) north of Victoria

Before the 1860s, the only connection Victoria had to the rest of Vancouver Island was by sea. In 1861, however, a rough trail, called the Goldstream Trail, was cut over the Malahat Ridge, connecting Parson's Bridge near Esquimalt Harbour with farms in the Cowichan Valley. The trail was only a few feet wide, however, suitable only for walking, riding horseback or driving livestock. In the mid-1880s, the trail was widened to accommodate wagons, but the easiest connection between Victoria and the rest of the island remained the water route because the steep trail over the Malahat was continually plagued with rocks, fallen trees and floods.

The first real road was built over the ridge after the turn of the century. Opening in the summer of 1911, the 10 miles (16 km) of road that was cut over and blasted through the ridge had to be rebuilt in 1925 and has undergone regular reconstruction since then. Today, though, the trip between Victoria and the Cowichan Valley, which took two or three days on the old Goldstream Trail, can be made in less than a half an hour.

Robert Service Writes First Poem
Cobble Hill Corner, Highway 1, 11 miles (18 km) north of Malahat Summit

Robert Service, the famed Yukon poet, was living the life of a hobo and part-time farmhand on the California coast when the Klondike Gold Rush began in 1897. By 1901, he had drifted north, where he found a job working on a farm 5 miles (8 km) east of the highway here. After working as a farmhand for a short time, Service was promoted to clerk in the store that operated on the farmstead. In addition to tending the store, Service also served as a part-time school teacher for the children of the farm. He also became known in the area for his acting abilities in the community's amateur theater group. It was while working and living here that Service submitted what is reported to have been his first published work. It was published in the *Duncan Enterprise* on December 5, 1903, and—written about the local swimming hole—already displayed the whimsical humor that made Service famous a few years later when he moved to the Yukon. In part, the poem reads

> He stands alone by the water's edge,
> With pale and anguished brow,
> And shudders as he murmurs low:
> "It must be done and now."
>
> . . .
>
> Through all his tense and rigid frame
> Great thrills of horror run;
> And once again he murmurs hoarse:
> "It must and shall be done."
>
> His mind made up. A long last look,
> A plunge, and all is o'er.
> He's taken —what was his intent—
> His morning bath—no more.

Settlers Stop Train at Duncan's Farm
E & N Railway Station, Highway 1, 18 miles (29 km) north of Malahat Summit, downtown Duncan

---

The Esquimalt & Nanaimo Railway began operation in 1886. Built by Robert Dunsmuir with several business partners, the last spike on the E & N was driven home by Prime Minister John A. Macdonald at a ceremony at Shawnigan Lake that August. Macdonald and Dunsmuir intended to address audiences of settlers along the route, so short stops also were planned in the Cowichan Valley at Koksilah and Somenos, a few miles south and north respectively from present-day Duncan. Both small settlements were slated for train depots.

But settlers around William C. Duncan's farm felt a station

was needed closer to their homes, and they gathered at a spot on Duncan's farm where the train was to pass by. Indians from the nearby Somenos Reserve also came to see the train. The assembly at Duncan grew to about 2,000 people, making it the largest of any along the route. A cedar and fir archway was built over the tracks, which along with the assembled crowd almost literally forced the train to make an unscheduled stop.

As the engine hissed and groaned and came to a stop, Macdonald and Dunsmuir emerged from a special car at the rear to address the crowd. A group of school children sang them a greeting, and a delegation of settlers presented them with a petition for a station near their farms. According to local legend, Dunsmuir didn't give an immediate answer. Instead, he waited until the last minute, and as the train was pulling away, announced that he would, indeed, build an E & N station on Duncan's farm. The station was constructed the following year, and the town of Duncan grew up around it.

Indian Leads Hudson's Bay Men to Nanaimo Coal
McKay Point, Newcastle Island, Highway 1, 40 miles (64 km) north of Duncan at Nanaimo

---

The City of Nanaimo originally grew up near coal mines established by the Hudson's Bay Company beginning in 1852. Discovery of the area's coal is usually credited to Joseph William McKay, for whom McKay Point on nearby Newcastle Island is named. In fact, however, the coal had been known to Nanaimo Indians for generations, and it was one of their tribe who showed McKay the rich deposits.

According to the story McKay himself later told, he first learned of the coal near this harbor when a Nanaimo Indian, later known as Coal Tyee, or Coal Chief, brought a broken rifle to the blacksmith at Fort Victoria for repair. While waiting for his gun to be fixed, Coal Chief examined some of the coal the blacksmith used to operate his forge. After a time he put the coal down and told the blacksmith that he knew where a lot more coal could be found. The blacksmith went to get McKay, a trader with the Hudson's Bay Company at that time. McKay told Coal Chief he would give him a bottle of rum and pay for the gun's repair if he would bring back some of the coal. Coal Chief said that he would, although McKay dismissed the matter when the Indian didn't come back to Fort Victoria all winter. The following spring, however, Coal Chief returned, and he brought McKay an entire canoe-load of coal. McKay then had Coal Chief lead him to the coal deposits.

According to the story, Coal Chief had first discovered coal at Nanaimo while digging clams. Because the coal was so light, he put some of it in a fire to see if it would burn. That's how he knew Nanaimo's coal was the same material the blacksmith used at Fort Victoria. Once the mines were opened, Nanaimo became the most important coal mining center on Vancouver Island for the Hudson's Bay Company. Coal from here replaced an inferior grade coal the company had been mining until that time at Fort Rupert, near today's Port Hardy.

First Jury Trial in West Hangs Indians
Nanaimo Harbour, Gallows Point, Nanaimo

Part of the mythology of Canada is that the rule of law came west with the settlers or even preceded them. The truth is that settlement progressed so slowly in Western Canada that by the time most of the settlers arrived in the late 1800s, law of one sort or another had, indeed, preceded them. Early on, however, the Canadian West was as lawless as anywhere else on the continent. Right and wrong, punishment and retribution were decided summarily by whoever wielded the most power. Courts of law were unheard of. Hudson's Bay Company officials dealt with murder by ignoring it if the victim was Indian. But if the supposed murderer was an Indian and the victim white, retribution was swift, brutal and deadly. Sometimes, if the killer himself couldn't be found, killing a relative or two of the Indian in question was considered close enough.

By 1853, however, Vancouver Island was officially a colony, not merely a preserve of the Hudson's Bay Company, so a show of legality by the Company of Adventurers became more important than before. It was in this year that British Columbia became the site of the first jury trial ever held in Western Canada. The jury was hardly one formed from the ranks of the accused's peers, however. The trial of two Indian men charged with the murder of a white man at a sheep station on the

Matthew Baillie Begbie, the colony of British Columbia's first judge.

Saanich Peninsula was composed entirely of officers of the Hudson's Bay Company, comrades of the slain man and subordinates of Governor James Douglas, who oversaw the trial and had the men arrested in the first place.

Not much is known about the murder. The victim was alone at the sheep station at the time, although a second man reported to Governor Douglas that he had seen Indians in the morning before he had gone to gather the sheep. Later, items stolen from the sheep station were found among the Cowichans, and the names of two Indians, one a Cowichan, the other the son of a Nanaimo chief, were given to Governor Douglas as the perpetrators of the crime. Douglas immediately dispatched the Hudson's Bay Company steamship *Beaver* to the region with a force of

Hudson's Bay Company employees and a Royal Navy warship to arrest the guilty parties.

The Indians, not surprisingly, did not wish to give up the accused men to the whites. But after negotiations that included threats of cannon fire and other retributions, the two Indians accused of the crime were finally turned over to Governor Douglas. A trial on board the *Beaver* was held immediately. The same afternoon a jury of Hudson's Bay Company officers declared the two Indians guilty. Assembling every member of the Nanaimo tribe in the area to watch the proceedings, Douglas had the two men hanged near the entrance of today's Nanaimo Harbour, at a spot on Protection Island now called Gallows Point. White man's law had come to British Columbia—although the Indians could be forgiven for not noticing much change.

Jack Dolholt Loses Mate but Gets His Ship Back
Jack Point, Nanaimo Harbour

Jack Point on Nanaimo Harbour was for about 40 years the home of Jack Dolholt, one of early Vancouver Island's more colorful characters. Perhaps the most famous Dolholt story concerns the time in December 1861 when, as captain of the *Victoria Packet,* he freighted passengers and cargo on an eventful run between Victoria and Saltspring Island. Before leaving Victoria, Dolholt had spent more than a little time drinking with his onboard assistant, a young man named Charlie. When the two reached their vessel, Captain Dolholt felt somewhat inadequate to the task of piloting his vessel to Saltspring, so he turned the wheel over to his mate.

Once out of Victoria Harbour, however, Dolholt decided he wanted his boat back. Charlie, in a mood of well-being equal to Dolholt's, gladly turned things over to the captain, but stumbling away from the wheel, he tripped over a coil of rope and fell overboard. Dolholt didn't hesitate. Forgetting his passengers and ship for the moment, he lowered a boat, and leaving the *Victoria Packet* to the fate of sea and weather, oared away to save his mate and companion.

Dolholt had no sooner left the vessel, however, than the passengers discovered they were adrift with no one at the helm. Fortunately, there were enough seaworthy souls among the passengers to run the craft safely aground at Ross Bay, where they anchored and went ashore. Meanwhile, Captain Dolholt gave up the search for his lost mate, who had, unfortunately, drowned. Catching up to the *Victoria Packet* at Ross Bay, Dolholt managed to convince two of his passengers to continue with him to Saltspring. Five others declined the trip and hiked back to Victoria to await passage on a less exciting vessel.

Deserters Flee to Gabriola
Gabriola Island, Strait of Georgia, opposite Nanaimo Harbour

Gabriola Island, like most of the other Gulf Islands, is home today to all sorts of people who have escaped their previous lives to take up residence on an idyllic island. It has been the scene of such escape attempts since the earliest days of its recorded history. In 1863, thirteen members of the crew of the Royal Navy's sloop *Chameleon,* including two petty officers, stole one of the ship's cutters in broad daylight and deserted His Majesty's service. Leaving Nanaimo Harbour under fire, they made for Gabriola Island.

A party of men was sent after them, but instead of hunting the deserters down in daylight the lieutenant in charge had the men row over to Gabriola late in the evening. Here, the men built a large fire along the shore and moved into the trees to hide. After a while, the deserters, lured by the fire, came out of the dark to stand around the apparently deserted fire. Eventually, they began cooking a supper for themselves. It was later reported that the men became quite jovial in the fire's glow, spending much of their time joking about their escape from the Royal Navy.

After a time, however, the men were arrested by their former comrades hiding in the trees. Back in Fort Victoria they were tried and found guilty of desertion. Their punishments could have been death, but the stiffest penalty any of them received was four years of penal servitude.

One Voter Sends Nanaimo Politician to Legislature
Bastion Street, Nanaimo

Ten years after the colony of Vancouver Island had been established, democracy was still an unwanted infant in Governor James Douglas's swiftly changing empire. The gold rush and subsequent immigration were already transforming the colony, pulling it from Douglas's control, but even as late as 1859 the old ways were still dominant. Under the Colonial Voting Act, only British citizens owning property worth at least 300 pounds (136 kg) were eligible to vote. In Nanaimo, that made Captain Charles E. Stuart the only voter. Stuart chose Captain John Swanson, a Douglas loyalist, to be his representative in Victoria, and the elections officer, Dr. Alfred Benson, for whom nearby Mt. Benson is named, duly noted that Swanson was "elected by a majority of one." Stuart had earlier elected one John Barnston of Victoria as his representative, but Barnston had failed to assume his seat, thus making the second election necessary.

Parks Settles in Park in Parksville
Junction of Highways 19 and 4, 18 miles (29 km) north of Nanaimo, Parksville

Until 1886 most people on this part of Vancouver Island simply called the small community located here The River. That year, however, Nelson Parks began running a new post office for the community out of his small log cabin. A post office needed a name, and Parks called his Parksville. No one had any better ideas, so soon everyone else in the community began calling the settlement Parksville, too. Today, the place where Parks had his cabin and opened the town's first post office is part of the community's large, downtown park.

Lieutenant Mayne First to Stop at Cathedral Grove
MacMillan Park, Highway 4, 17.5 miles (28 km) west of Parksville and Highway 19

In the early days of settlement on Vancouver Island, the rugged geography of the region often made roads impossible even between nearby communities. Port Alberni, like most coastal communities in the 1860s, was connected to the outside world only by sea. When Adam Grant Horne crossed overland from Nanaimo to Alberni Canal in 1856, he found no easily accessible trail. In 1859, Captain George Richards attempted to find a route suitable for a wagon road between Alberni and Qualicum, but he, too, was unsuccessful.

Still, Governor James Douglas was convinced there must be a suitable way across the mountains and forests that could serve as an accessible east–west trail across the island. In 1861, he asked Lieutenant Richard Mayne, for whom today's Mayne Island is named, to find a route between Alberni and Nanaimo. Mayne set out with Indian packers and guides in April, traveling over a trail that closely follows the present highway between Port Alberni and Coombs. At first, though, he cut more southeasterly than today's highway and proceeded to Nanoose Bay, where he followed the coast to Nanaimo.

Mayne took two weeks to make a round trip. At a point where his route passed through Cathedral Grove in today's MacMillan Park, Mayne's records show that he and his men stopped to rest under a huge tree. In all likelihood, visitors to the park today can rest under that same tree after a convenient drive from either Nanaimo or Port Alberni. After his two weeks on the trail, however, Lieutenant Mayne decided that no route over the terrain between Port Alberni and Nanaimo was suitable for road construction, not even for a primitive wagon trail. He recommended to Governor Douglas that no such trail ever be attempted.

Sproat Starts Sawmill
Highway 4, 29 miles (46.5 km) west of junction with Highway 19, Port Alberni

Port Alberni came into being in 1860 when Gilbert Malcolm Sproat and eight other men came ashore here and to build a sawmill. The settlement was given its name the following year by Captain Richards of the HMS *Hecate,* acknowledging the Spanish explorers who explored and mapped the inlet 70 years earlier. After leaving Alberni, Sproat went on to serve the British Columbia government in several positions, becoming the province's first agent general in London in 1872 and acting as Indian land commissioner in the Kootenays in the 1880s. Sproat Falls and Lake, 5 miles (8 km) west of Port Alberni, are named in his honor.

Tay Fire Burns Forest
Highway 4, 40 miles (64 km) west of Port Alberni

Burned snags still seen in the replanted forest here are the remains of the Tay Fire, which burned 10 square miles (26 square km) of forest in August 1967. The Tay Fire started as a result of road construction during the building of today's highway. After the fire, the planting of the trees you see growing here began almost immediately and continued for 10 years. Despite the fire, almost 70 percent of the blackened but still intact trees were harvested by forest companies between 1967 and 1972.

Florencia Wrecked Three Times
Florencia Bay, Long Beach, Pacific Rim National Park, Willowbrae Road parking lot, 1 mile (1.6 km) south of Highway 4, Ucluelet junction, 60 miles (96.5 km) west of Port Alberni

Florencia Bay is named after the *Peruvian* shipwrecked off this point in 1860. The *Florencia*, under Captain J.P. de Echiandeia, sailed from Utsalady, Washington, carrying a cargo of lumber and three passengers on November 8. She was blown onto her side in a gale off Cape Flattery on November 12. Because she was loaded with lumber, the *Florencia* floated on her side for a time, but then righted herself, bouncing about in the storm. Her deck cargo, mainmast and fore-top-mast, along with the Captain, the cook and a passenger had been lost in the sea, but the *Florencia* attempted to fight the storm once again, half sailing and half drifting into Nootka Sound where she took anchor.

Word of her troubles was brought to Victoria by the yacht *Templar,* and the British gunboat *Forward* was immediately sent to her rescue. Meanwhile, at Nootka, the *Florencia* was pumped out and found to be tight. As well, word came of the sinking of the American brig *Consort* at nearby San Josef Bay. When the *Forward* arrived she went first to pick up survivors from the *Consort,* then took the *Florencia* in tow, intending to return to Victoria.

After a short way, however, the *Forward* had an accident in one of its boilers and, deeming the *Florencia* sufficiently seaworthy, cut her adrift. The *Forward* then headed back to Nootka for repairs while the *Florencia* attempted to sail southeast for the Strait of Juan de Fuca. Once more, however, the *Florencia* encountered gale force winds and, though attempting to make the strait for several days, was eventually run aground at a point south of here known today, in the *Florencia's* honor, as Wreck Bay.

Pass of Melfort Smashed at Amphitrite Point
Amphitrite Point Lighthouse, 6 miles (9.5 km) southeast of junction of Highway 4 and Ucluelet/Tofino Road, Ucluelet

Just a quarter mile (.4 km) east of the lighthouse here the *Pass of Melfort* sank after being driven against the rocks on December 26, 1905. The *Pass of Melfort* was bound for Puget Sound when caught in a southeast gale, driven north in the storm and tossed against the rocky shoreline, where she was smashed to pieces in a matter of hours. All 36 people aboard were killed. Ironically, her skipper, Captain Cougall, had come out of retirement to sail the *Pass of Melfort* on one last voyage. He had agreed to sail the vessel only as a favor to his old shipping company after the previous captain had been fired for drunkenness and the company had been unable to find a replacement.

Captain Cougall came aboard the *Pass of Melfort* at Panama and sailed for the northwest coast. On his way to Port Townsend, he encountered a storm off the west coast of Washington State. Southeast squalls then carried his ship up the coast of Vancouver Island. It appears from some of the recovered wreckage that Captain Cougall and the *Pass of Melfort* had somehow rescued seven survivors from the derelict *King of David,* a ship that had been destroyed in a storm farther north on Banjo Reef. These men, too, already lost and saved once, were lost again in the storm with the others aboard the *Pass of Melfort.* As a result of the tragedy, work began on a lighthouse at Amphitrite Point soon after the incident. The first structure was later destroyed by a tidal wave on January 2, 1914, but was rebuilt immediately.

Meares Builds First House and Sparks International Incident
Meares Island, Tofino Inlet, east of Tofino, 21 miles (38 km) northwest of junction of Highway 4 and Tofino/Ucluelet Road

Meares Island is named for Captain John Meares, who first came to the British Columbia coast in 1786. After successfully trading with Indians at Nootka and selling the furs back in China, Meares returned to Vancouver Island in 1788. This time he obtained land at Friendly Cove on Nootka Island from Maquinna, the hereditary chief of the Nootka. Meares used the land to build a storehouse, which became the first European-style building erected in what eventually became the province of British Columbia. Meares had brought 70 Chinese immigrants with him to work at his new post—the first immigrants to arrive in British Columbia. After they built his fur post, he put them to work building the first sailing vessel built on the north Pacific coast, which he called the *North West America*.

After Meares returned again to China to sell furs, Don Estevan Jose Martinez arrived at Nootka from San Blas, Mexico. Martinez had come north to reassert Spanish control in the Pacific Northwest, and the first thing he did after he arrived was confiscate Meares's property, citing Spain's right to the area by right of prior discovery. Martinez seized the *North West America* and a second vessel belonging to Meares, conscripted Meares's Chinese workers to build his own residence and confiscated a large quantity of furs. When this news reached Meares in China, he immediately left for London, where he petitioned the members of the House of Commons to redress his grievances.

Discounting all Spanish claims to the Pacific Northwest, the British parliament immediately voted funds to prepare a large fleet for war. It also demanded that Spain reimburse Meares a huge sum of money for his losses at Nootka and the subsequent trade he might otherwise have enjoyed in China. Faced with imminent British violence against them, Spain backed down and signed the first Nootka Accord in 1790. This accord resulted in a joint British and Spanish presence at Nootka until the Spanish withdrew from the area entirely a few years later.

Tonquin Destroyed by Sailor in Indian Battle
Clayoquot Sound

Clayoquot Sound, lying to the north of Tofino on the northern side of Vargas Island, was the scene of one of the bloodiest Indian battles ever fought on the northwest coast. In 1811, the American ship *Tonquin* lay at anchor off Village Harbour. Jonathan Thorn was the ship's captain. Alexander McKay was the chief trader. Thorn had been a U.S. navy hero in the recent war with Tripoli, but his disciplinarian style and rigid notions of proper conduct made him poorly suited for the Indian trade. It was Thorn, in fact, who sparked a dispute that caused the death of over 200 Clayoquot Indians and every member of his crew except one.

One afternoon, in the midst of trading, Thorn grew angry at the Clayoquot chief, Nookamis, for his constant haggling over prices. In one impulsive moment Thorn grabbed a pelt from Nookamis's hands and rubbed it angrily across the Indian's face, a gesture not surprisingly regarded by the Clayoquot chief as a terrible insult. McKay, an experienced trader, advised Thorn to set sail immediately after the incident. But Thorn, arrogant and prejudiced, dismissed any possibility that a band of Indians, unschooled in European ways, could out-fight white sailors. Not only did Thorn choose to stay in the sound, he refused to take any extra precautions against Indian attack.

The next morning, Indians, as usual, were allowed to come on board to trade. All were admitted, even the young Clayoquot war chief, Shewish. Nookamis seemed particularly friendly, with no sign of the bickering over prices that had marked his behavior the day before. All of the Indians seemed particularly interested in trading furs for knives, and great profits were quickly made by the white traders.

Suddenly, Shewish gave a signal for the attack, and the Indians, who outnumbered the whites, began wielding their newly purchased knives. The sailor James Lewis was one of the first to be wounded. Left for dead, Lewis climbed to the rigging to escape the battle raging below. The entire crew was soon killed, except for four sailors who managed to escape in the rigging with Lewis.

These five men managed to slip down the ropes and get into the ship's cabin, where they obtained a sufficient supply of loaded muskets to return to the deck and, guns blazing, drive off the Indians. The men knew their victory would be short-lived, however, and decided to slip away from the ship in a dinghy under cover of darkness. The wounded Lewis opposed this plan and refused to go, so the other four left without him. Before morning arrived, they were captured and killed by the Clayoquot.

The next morning Lewis embarked on a plan of his own.

Before light he prepared kegs of gunpowder below deck. When all was ready, he went up on deck to show himself to the Indians on shore. Shewish, the war chief, and his warriors took to their canoes to retake the ship. When they came on board, however, Lewis could not be found. The Indians gave the matter little thought as they began looting the ship. Finally, with more than 200 Clayoquot people on board, Lewis, from his hiding place, lit a fuse, and moments later the ship exploded, sending debris and people, wounded and dead, into the water.

The *Tonquin* was completely destroyed. Lewis, of course, was among them. It took years for the events of the tragedy to be pieced together, but the Indian interpreter captured by the Clayoquots, the Indians themselves, and one of their slaves who later lived at Fort Langley all filled in parts of the tale that finally revealed what had happened to Captain Thorn and the ill-fated *Tonquin*.

RETURNING TO HIGHWAY 19 AT PARKSVILLE

Town Not Named for Dog Bartender
Highway 19, 21 miles (38 km) north of Highway 4, Bowser

The little settlement of Bowser, despite some stories, was not named after a dog. The town was named for former British Columbia Premier W.J. Bowser. Nevertheless, the town of Bowser did have a famous dog.

Back in the 1930s, the Winfield family, who owned the Bowser Hotel, trained their dog to deliver beer to patrons of the hotel's beer parlor. According to reports that ranged as far afield as *Ripley's Believe It Or Not*, the dog, providentially named Bowser, would carry a bottle of beer in his mouth to whatever table he was told. When he delivered the beer he would wait and collect money from whoever took the bottle, then return to the bar, where his master would collect the cash. Bowser never did learn to use the cash register. If change was required, the human bartender would count it out, and then give it to Bowser to take back to the table where he'd delivered the beer. According to Revenue Canada, Bowser's tips were never recorded on his income tax returns.

Wild Bunch Gang Member Captured at Union Bay
Highway 19, 15 miles (24 km) north of Bowser, Union Bay

A brutal encounter between British Columbia police officers and a pair of thieves at Union Bay in 1913 resulted in the arrest of Henry Wagoner, one of the American West's most notorious outlaws. Also known as the Flying Dutchman, Wagoner had been a member of the Wild Bunch with Butch Cassidy and the Sundance Kid when the gang used to hide out in Wyoming's Hole-in-the-Wall country. When Cassidy and Sundance escaped to South America and the American cavalry broke up the gang at Hole-in-the-Wall, Wagoner escaped with a few other gang members and continued a life in crime farther west.

Finally arrested in Washington State, he spent 14 years in the penitentiary in Walla Walla. Immediately after his release, though, he tried to rob a post office and killed a county sheriff in the process. Along with another former Wild Bunch gang member, Bill Julian, Wagoner stole the motorized MS *Spray* at Gray's Harbour on Puget Sound and escaped to the British Columbia coast.

In the months that followed, the British Columbia provincial police noted a pattern of robberies developing in the Gulf Islands, several small logging communities on the east side of Vancouver Island and the larger coal-shipping center at Union Bay. The cycle always began with a series of thefts in the Gulf Islands, moved to coastal logging communities and finally to the big haul at Union Bay.

As police officers noted the cycle repeating itself, moving once more toward a major robbery at Union Bay, a pair of young officers, Harry Westaway and Gordon Ross, was sent to the community to beef up the protection normally provided by a lone policeman, Constable "Big Mac" McKenzie. Westaway and Ross were assigned to patrol the town at night and offer any other assistance they could to McKenzie.

Shortly after midnight on March 3, 1913, as the two new men patrolled the town, they noticed a flash of light in the Fraser & Bishop store on main street. Ross was unarmed, but he still rushed with Westaway to the store. Opening the building's side door, the two young constables cast a lamp beam over the room. A shot rang out and Ross felt a bullet graze his shoulder. Then he heard a thud as the shot, after tearing through his skin, struck his partner in the chest.

Without hesitation and with only the nightstick for protection, Ross dived for the spot where the flash of gunfire had exploded. Tackling the gunman and wielding his nightstick, Ross realized he was in a fight for his life with a man as big or bigger than he was. Ross grabbed first for the robber's gun hand, but the man wrenched his wrist from Ross's grip and began pummeling him with the gun butt. At the same time the man's other hand went to Ross's throat, choking him until he couldn't breathe.

Ross still had fight left, however, and as the gunman beat his head with the gun, Ross hit the thief with his nightstick hard enough to knock him over. Finally gaining the upper hand, Ross hit the man over and over until the desperado finally fell and didn't get up. Soon afterward, Constable McKenzie arrived. By then, Constable Westaway was dead. Later, it was learned the man they had arrested was the famous Flying Dutchman, Henry Wagoner, of Butch Cassidy's Wild Bunch. Police captured Bill Julian—who had escaped from the store while Ross and Wagoner were struggling—on Lasquetti Island the following day. After a brief trial, Wagoner, one of the last of the Wild West's most brutal desperadoes, was hanged.

Ginger Goodwin Shot at Cumberland
Highway 19, Royston Road, 6.5 miles (10.5 km) north of Union Bay

Five miles (8 km) east on Royston Road from this corner is the old mining town of Cumberland. Coal hasn't been mined in Cumberland since the 1960s, but in the years just after the turn of the century the seven mines at Cumberland proved to be some of the most lucrative on Vancouver Island. Cumberland's mines also sparked some of the fiercest labor disputes in British Columbia, a province with a long history of labor unrest.

Indians knew about the coal at Cumberland for years and began telling whites of its existence as early as the 1850s, but it wasn't until 1869 that a group of Nanaimo miners attempted to work the deposit commercially. When the miners couldn't come up with enough cash to open a mine, however, Robert Dunsmuir, already well on his way to becoming the richest man in British Columbia, bought up the claims. He built a railroad from the mines to the coast at Union Bay and began hiring miners by the hundreds.

Dunsmuir's mines were profitable, but they also were dangerous, and he paid his workers poorly. Between 1884 and 1912, 373 men were killed at Cumberland mines. In 1912, the disgruntled miners went on strike. The following year the strike against the Dunsmuir coal empire spread to Nanaimo and acting Premier W.J. Bowser sent in soldiers to keep the mines open with nonstriking employees, many of them Chinese immigrants threatened with deportation if they walked out.

Several years later, during World War I, Albert "Ginger" Goodwin, a prominent member of the labor movement who had been active in the Cumberland strike, fled to the Cumberland area after the government attempted to draft him into the Canadian army. Goodwin at first claimed ill-health, but then skipped out. Local police soon discovered his hiding place in the hills behind Cumberland, and on July 26, 1918, Goodwin was shot and killed. Police claimed he was resisting arrest. Others claimed he was murdered because of his involvement in the Cumberland strike and other labor movement activities. On August 2, miners organized the first general strike in Canadian history to honor Goodwin's memory.

Indians Unimpressed with Captain Courtenay
Highway 19, 11 miles (18 km) north of Union Bay, Courtenay

The town of Courtenay was named for Captain George William Courtenay, commander of the HMS *Constance,* which patrolled the northwest coast from 1846 to 1849. In the early years of Fort Victoria, when Chief Factor Roderick Finlayson strove to impress the Indians of the region with the military superiority of the British, Courtenay was asked to bring a contingent of his Royal Marines ashore to put on a demonstration. The marines were called to the parade grounds, where they participated in several military exercises while the Indians looked on.

Afterward, Courtenay asked a prominent Songhee chief what he thought of the fighting power of the British. The chief asked Courtenay if his soldiers always fought in the open like they had done in the demonstrations. Courtenay answered in the affirmative. The chief shook his head and said that he thought it would be smarter to fight from behind trees and rocks like the Songhee. Courtenay was never asked to repeat his demonstration for the Indians.

Quadra and Vancouver Island Proved to be Island
Highway 19, 28 miles (45 km) north of Highway 28, Courtenay, Campbell River

When Captain George Vancouver set out to map the British Columbia coast in 1792, he had no idea if the land we now know as Vancouver Island was really an island. In fact, after entering the Strait of Juan de Fuca, Vancouver named the large body of water leading north the Gulf of Georgia rather than the strait because he assumed that the yet-to-be-named Vancouver Island was indeed part of the mainland. Even after sailing as far north as Desolation Sound, Vancouver didn't know for sure how much farther north he would be able to sail before reaching the top of his "gulf." Vancouver fully expected to have to backtrack out the mouth of the Strait of Juan de Fuca to get to the west side of Vancouver Island and Nootka Island, where he was to meet with the Spanish commander Don Juan Francisco de la Bodega y Quadra.

To settle the matter, Vancouver sent four of his lieutenants—Johnstone, Swaine, Puget and Whidbey—to explore the surrounding territory. Johnstone and Swaine found an outlet into today's Johnstone Strait through Yaculta Rapids. Puget and Whidbey traveled up the east coast of Vancouver Island to Discovery Passage and, on July 3, anchored off today's Campbell River. Here, the strong tides in Discovery Passage convinced them that the channel had to lead back to the open sea. The two men took this news back to Captain Vancouver. Combined with the news Johnstone brought back, Vancouver determined that Discovery Passage would be the safest and fastest route for completing the circumnavigation of what was now known to be an island.

Once back at Nootka, it was Quadra who suggested to Vancouver that they should name some geographical point after themselves. Vancouver liked the idea and offered to call the newly confirmed island Quadra and Vancouver Island. Quadra thought that had a ring to it, and the name was entered on both Spanish and English charts. But the name proved to be too long for cartographers, and by the mid-1800s maps were already showing a simple Vancouver Island where once the two names had stood. To rectify this injustice somewhat, the name Quadra was later given to the large island opposite Campbell River.

Instant Town Springs to Life
Highway 28, 53 miles (85 km) west of Campbell River, Gold River

The community of Gold River didn't evolve as most towns do. It was built all at once in the summer of 1965 after the province of British Columbia passed legislation to allow incorporation of what was dubbed at the time "instant towns." Instant towns were company towns built to accommodate workers in remote areas where new mines, mills or some other form of frontier industry was developed. Gold River, the first town incorporated after the legislation was passed, was built for workers at the nearby Thasis Pulp Mill on Muchalat Inlet. Ironically, Gold River, one of British Columbia's newest towns, is only a few miles up the inlet from Nootka Sound, where Captain John Meares brought British Columbia's first immigrants to work at his fur post in 1788, thus establishing British Columbia's first nonaboriginal town.

First European Contact with Vancouver Island Indians
28 miles (45 km) southwest of Gold River, Estavan Point

Europeans' first contact with the native people on Vancouver Island occurred in early August 1774 southwest of Gold River off Estavan Point at the entrance to Nootka Sound. Juan Josef Perez Hernandez, commanding the Spanish frigate *Santiago* had sailed north that spring with orders to reach the 60th parallel in waters off today's Alaskan Panhandle. Perez had come to investigate Russian claims and influence in the Northwest, to make suitable claims along the coast for Spain and make whatever contact he could with the native people of the northwest coast.

The geography of the region, particularly the treacherous Inside Passage, made Perez nervous, however, and he stayed as far as he could from the jagged shorelines. By the time he reached the 55th parallel, he was so concerned for the welfare of his ship in the sometimes narrow, uncharted channels of the northern reaches of the passage that he turned back. Perez saw nothing of the Russians on his voyage. He claimed no new territory for Spain, but twice on his journey south he did make con-

Totems at Alert Bay.

tact with native people; or rather, native people made contact with him.

On July 18, through a mist-clouded rain, Perez and the crew of the *Santiago* came within sight of the Queen Charlotte Islands. Although they made no attempt to go ashore, a few days later as the *Santiago* sailed slowly down the coast, Haida canoed out to make contact with their European visitors. A small amount of trading was completed by lowering and raising items over the *Santiago*'s side to reach one of the Indian canoes. It was noted that one of the Indians carried a harpoon with an iron point, probably traded by the Russians to a Tlingit, who later traded it to the Haida. The next day more trading was undertaken before the *Santiago* again headed south.

On August 8, now lying near Estavan Point near the entrance of Nootka Sound, Perez made his second contact with native people. Once again he was too timid to go ashore, but a band of Nootka from today's Hesquiat Harbour came out to visit him. Nootka legend suggests the people feared that the Spanish ship might contain avenging spirits, and perhaps that's why the Nootka did not immediately embrace their European visitors. All during the day and into the night, Indians howled and sang mournful songs in the water near the *Santiago*. When nothing happened that night, however, about 100 of the Indians returned to the *Santiago* and traded what they could to the

Spanish, mostly for abalone shells, silver utensils and iron tools.

From this brief contact Spain based its claims to territory on the northwest coast. Four years later, in March 1778, James Cook sailed his ship into Nootka Sound and established a British claim to the area. The region was so infrequently visited at the time, however, that no conflict developed between the two countries until the late 1780s. Eventually, a joint occupation of the Northwest was established by the Nootka Treaty of 1790 and by the joint exploration of the territory by British and Spanish ships under the commands of George Vancouver and Don Juan Francisco de la Bodega y Quadra.

By the 1790s, Spanish power in North America was on the decline, and in the summer of 1795, the Spanish flag was lowered at their fort at Friendly Cove, which they called Puerto de la Santa Cruz. No formal retreat was ever made from the area, but the Spanish never went back. Today, a small granite monolith on the site bears the inscription, "Vancouver and Quadra met here in August, 1792, under the treaty between Spain and Great Britain of October, 1790. Erected by the Washington State Historical Society, August, 1903."

Indians Hanged for Murders Never Committed
31 miles (50 km) southwest of Gold River, Hesquiat Harbour

Southwest of Gold River, and just south of Estavan Point in the open sea at the top of Hesquiat Harbour, the bark *John Bright,* with a load of lumber bound for South America, was wrecked during a heavy southwest gale in February 1869. All on board were killed, but it was never known if the passengers and crew members perished in the storm or if some survivors were later murdered by Hesquiat Indians once they reached shore.

News of the shipwreck didn't arrive in Victoria until early in March, when Captain Christensen of the schooner *Surprise* brought news of mutilated bodies found on Hesquiat Peninsula. The HMS *Sparrowhawk* was sent north to investigate. It found and buried the bodies and returned with seven Hesquiat prisoners. The Indians were put on trial for murder, even though they claimed they had not killed or mutilated anyone and there was no direct evidence linking them to the killings. They said that the bodies had washed ashore, where they were beaten against the rocks in the surf until the Indians had dragged them above the waterline so they wouldn't be eaten by fish.

Nevertheless, all seven were found guilty. In July, they were taken back to Hesquiat Harbour. A gallows was constructed and all of the Indians of the area were gathered to witness the executions. The Indians were required to attend because it was felt they should all witness the punishment for murdering whites. To this day, Hesquiat accounts maintain that the only murders committed here were by the white authorities who falsely accused Indians and then hanged them for crimes they did not commit.

Maquinna Takes Two Prisoners During Slaughter on Trading Ship *Boston*
Nootka Island

In 1803, the trading vessel *Boston*, out of that city, was engaged in the Nootka trade here when Captain John Slater made the fatal mistake of insulting the Nootka Chief Maquinna. Maquinna had returned a shotgun that Slater had given him. The gun had a broken lock, and Maquinna said it was *peshak*, or "no good." Slater, not realizing Maquinna spoke English, took back the gun while calling the chief a string of bad names for the benefit of the crew.

Maquinna left the ship in silent outrage. The next day Maquinna arranged to guide a party from the *Boston* on a fishing expedition to supply it with salmon. Nine men under the chief mate departed with their Indian guides, leaving the *Boston* with only a few men on board. About an hour later the Indians attacked. John Jewitt, the ship's armorer, heard a commotion on deck and climbed the ladder to see what was going on. As he reached the deck, an Indian grabbed him by the hair and slashed his forehead with an ax.

Jewitt fell, stunned and bleeding, into the steerage. When he regained consciousness, Maquinna ordered his warriors to spare his life because of his usefulness as a gunsmith. Jewitt was brought up on deck, where he found the heads of the *Boston*'s captain and crew members lined up in a row along a railing. Jewitt was told to name the man each of the heads had belonged to. About this time, a second survivor, an old man named Thompson, who served as the ship's sailmaker, was found hiding below deck. Jewitt told Maquinna that Thompson was his father and that he wouldn't be able to work if anything happened to him, so Maquinna allowed Thompson to live as well.

Jewitt and Thompson spent the next two years as captives of the Nootka. They probably survived only because they were the personal slaves of Maquinna. In a book Jewitt later wrote about his time with the Nootka, he relates how the two men were at first often insulted by the Indians and treated with contempt. Then one day Thompson killed an Indian visiting from a nearby band. Jewitt said the Indian had walked across a blanket Thompson had laid out to dry in the sun after washing it for Maquinna. The Indian purposely made the blanket dirty, and Thompson, who still carried his cutlass, told him that if he did it again he would cut off his head. The Indian walked across the blanket again, and Thompson, with one swift slash of the cutlass, cut off the man's head. He then wrapped the head in the blanket and took it to Maquinna.

Thompson and Jewitt had no idea what would happen to them when Thompson's crime was reported, but Maquinna, when he saw the head, merely laughed. From then on the two *Boston* sailors were never bothered by the other Indians. They did, whenever the occasion arose, try to smuggle word of their plight to the other trading vessels that continued to supply the Indians of the coast. Finally, after two years, word of their plight reached Captain Samuel Hill of the trading ship *Lydia*. Hill came to Nootka on July 19, 1905, and lured Maquinna on board with promises of presents. Once on board, Captain Hill captured Maquinna and held him in ransom for the lives of Jewitt and Thompson.

Blanket Bill Stiffs Governor Douglas
Nootka Island

In 1846, William Robert Jarman of the trading ship *Platypus* happened to be the only man ashore when Nootka warriors attacked the ship at Nootka Sound. The captain ordered the crew to set sail rather than fight the Nootka, and Bill Jarman was left to fend for himself.

Jarman didn't last long, however, and as soon as the Nootka captured him, he found himself the object of an argument between the Nootka chief, Maquinna, and his brother. The brother wanted to kill the white man immediately, but Maquinna wanted Jarman for a slave. They could always kill the white man later.

For two years Bill Jarman labored as the chief's slave and found that he fitted easily into Indian life. He was given two Indian wives and found that even as a slave he lived a leisurely life. Finally, however, word of Jarman's plight reached Governor Douglas in Victoria. Douglas arranged to ransom Jarman for a stack of Hudson's Bay Company blankets as tall as Jarman, who, Douglas made clear, would work off the debt so incurred as a temporary employee of the company at Fort Victoria. Once Jarman was brought to the fur post, everybody called him Blanket Bill because of the blankets that had obtained his freedom and also because a Nootka cedar blanket happened to be the only clothing he owned at the time he was ransomed.

Blanket Bill was happy to be free of his captors at first, but he soon tired of the regimen of regular employment at Fort Victoria. After about a week, he stole a canoe and under cover of night paddled across the Strait of Juan de Fuca to the American side, leaving his debt to the Hudson's Bay Company unpaid. Jarman lived on the American side in a Clallam village, where he married an Indian woman and slipped quietly into the native way of life once more. He joined the gold rush for a while, traded regularly with his Indian neighbors and occasionally worked for the American army at Fort Bellingham.

It was there, in 1857, that Captain Pickett asked Blanket Bill Jarman to pilot the fort's whaling boat to Victoria, where he and another officer planned to pay a visit to Governor Douglas. Although Blanket Bill stayed with the boat on the Victoria side Captain Pickett happened to mention to Governor Douglas that a man named Jarman had taken them across the strait. Douglas immediately remembered Blanket Bill and the debt, so he asked to speak to the Captain's employee. Sure enough, it was Blanket Bill, and Douglas proceeded to reprimand him for running out on his debt, explaining to Pickett what had happened to Jarman 10 years earlier. No record remains to confirm or deny that Blanket Bill paid Governor Douglas the money he was owed.

RETURNING TO HIGHWAY 19

Ripple Rock Blows its Top
Highway 19, 6 miles (10 km) north of Campbell River, Historical Stop of Interest Sign

The explosion at Ripple Rock, April 5, 1958.

Ripple Rock used to sit in the middle of the entrance to Seymour Narrows. The huge, double-headed rock, lying in wait just below the surface at low tide, was responsible for more than 100 shipwrecks. From the time Captain George Vancouver first found his way past Ripple in 1792, ships sailing the Inside Passage used to wait on the tide to avoid the rock, which came within 10' (3 m) of the surface during low tide. Then, in 1958, the Canadian government and 34 boxcar-loads of dynamite blew Ripple Rock down to size. It was one of the largest nonnuclear explosions in the history of the world.

To blow up Ripple, engineers drilled a shaft from nearby Maude Island. The shaft ran beneath the seabed and then turned up into the rock. The drilling and preparation took two and half years and more than $3 million dollars, but finally, on April 5,

1958, all was ready. The explosion lifted the surface of Seymour Narrows, sending an estimated 700,000 pounds (317,520 kg) of rock and water into the air and leaving a clearance of 47' (14 m)— safe passage for today's ships traveling the Inside Passage.

Strange Case of Amor De Cosmos
Highway 19, 22 miles (35 km) north of Campbell River, Amor De Cosmos Creek

Amor De Cosmos Creek takes its name from the eccentric but influential early proponent of democracy in British Columbia. De Cosmos also was the province's second premier. By popular sentiment at the time, De Cosmos probably should have been the first, but after the province joined Canada in 1871, De Cosmos's old opponents from colonial days, in consort with Canadian Prime Minister John A. Macdonald, saw to it that the honor went instead to John Foster McCreight. McCreight was a rather humorless lawyer without political experience or natural aptitude, whom his backers knew they could easily control.

De Cosmos led the opposition, but he did so somewhat distractedly. In addition to having a seat in the provincial legislature, he also was a member of parliament in the federal government representing the new Province of British Columbia. Despite De Cosmos's extended absences from Victoria, the McCreight government fell within two years, and De Cosmos succeeded to the premiership. After 15 years of leading the government's opposition on Vancouver Island and in British Columbia, De Cosmos was finally in charge. Despite his long wait, he proved better at opposing than governing.

Partly, this was the result of his dual role as premier of British Columbia and member of parliament in the national government. De Cosmos was only in British Columbia for part of the first session of his own government before he had to leave for Ottawa in the early spring of 1873. Ideologically, De Cosmos was more or less a Liberal. But in Ottawa he nevertheless aligned himself most closely with the Conservatives in his attempts to wring concessions for British Columbia from the national government.

In February 1874, after a new law prevented politicians from simultaneously serving in both provincial and federal governments, De Cosmos resigned as premier and gave up his seat in

Amor De Cosmos, British Columbia's second premier.

the provincial assembly in order to remain a member of parliament in Ottawa.

He was reelected to parliament twice more, but after repeated criticism resulting from his almost constant attempts to make the Canadian government more democratic, he was defeated in the election of 1883 by just 232 votes.

A bachelor, and always somewhat reclusive for a politician, De Cosmos returned to Victoria after his defeat. Here, he lived out his retirement, with his continuing eccentricities gradually becoming evidence of true and sometimes violent insanity.

Helmcken Island Always in Opposition
Highway 19, 45 miles (72 km) north of Campbell River, northeast of Sayward in Johnstone Strait, Sayward

In 1850, John Sebastian Helmcken, the Hudson's Bay Company doctor at Fort Victoria, traveled aboard the Hudson's Bay Company steamer *Beaver* through Johnstone Strait on his way to Fort Rupert. As he passed by Salmon Bay, near today's town of Sayward, Helmcken noticed that the *Beaver* had to buck a small island that increased the flood tide where the island compressed the waters of the strait into a channel on either side.

"What's the name of that island?" Helmcken asked the *Beaver*'s Captain Dodd. Dodd replied that they hadn't yet bothered to name it, but that since it always seemed to be in opposition they might as well call it Helmcken in honor of the doctor's contrary ways. Dodd continued to call it Helmcken and the name stuck. Four years later, when Dr. Helmcken became speaker of the Colonial Legislature, Captain Pender of the Royal Navy also named a large rock off the east end of Helmcken Island in the doctor's honor. He called the stone Speaker Rock.

Num-hyala-gi-yu Stirs Water
Highway 19, 9 miles north of Sayward Junction, Nimpkish River Bridge

Nimpkish River was first visited by Captain Vancouver in 1792, when he stopped and drew a sketch of an Indian village about 2 miles (3.2 km) downstream from here at the mouth of the river. Vancouver described the village as a populous settlement headed by a chief named Cheslakees. The village, called Whulk by its inhabitants, was still there in 1860, when Captain Richards of the HMS *Plumper* revisited the area and named the river. According to Richards, the village looked virtually the same as in Vancouver's nearly 70-year-old sketch.

The river's name comes from the *Num-hyala-gi-yu*, a mythological fish of the Kwakiutl that is so large the motion of its tail and fins causes huge waves. The fish was said to lie on the ocean bottom at the mouth of the river they called *Num-hyala-gi-yup-kish* in the Kwakwala language, which to Richards's European ears, sounded like Numpkish. When disturbed, the great fish would swim around and cause riptides. About 1870, Whulk's residents moved to Alert Bay on Cormorant Island, but remains of the terraces where the village houses stood can still be found on the west bank of the river.

"Go-To-Hell" McNeill Goes His Own Way
Highway 19, 84 miles (135 km) north of Sayward Junction, Port McNeill

Officers of the Hudson's Bay Company named Port McNeill in 1837 after William Henry McNeill, a Boston trader who was a major irritation to Hudson's Bay Company officials in the early 1830s. He first turned up on the northwest coast in the late spring of 1831 in command of the American brig *Llama*. McNeill sold his entire cargo that summer to the Hudson's Bay Company. Afterward, McNeill traded along the coast on his own.

Intent on preserving its monopoly in the region, the Hudson's Bay Company began pressuring McNeill to move on. In McNeill, however, the company found a particularly stubborn competitor who refused to be bullied. At one point, the Boston seafarer even turned to arms when he drove off the Hudson's Bay Company's ship *Cadboro* when it attempted to interfere with his trading.

Company officials quickly changed tactics. If McNeill couldn't be bullied, perhaps he could be bought. A deal was quickly made for the company to buy McNeill's vessel and hire McNeill as its captain. This arrangement worked so well that McNeill continued to work for the company in other capacities after he left his vessel. In 1837, he became captain of the Hudson's Bay Company's most famous coastal trading vessel, the steamship *Beaver*. The same year, he explored the south shore of Vancouver Island near today's Victoria and reported to the company that "there was an excellent harbour and a fine open country along the sea shore, apparently well adapted for both tillage and pasturage. . . ."

According to company governor George Simpson, McNeill was popular with the Indians he traded with, but they had a hard time pronouncing his name. The best they could do was something resembling "Ma-ta-heil." When McNeill would visit the coastal communities to trade, the Indians would begin chanting "Ma-ta-heil" over and over as soon as they saw him. The resulting chorus always sounded as if the Indians were chanting, "Go to hell." Or perhaps McNeill wasn't as popular as he was led to believe and the Indians really were chanting, "Go to hell."

First Co-op Store Organized at Sointula Utopian Community
Malcolm Island Ferry from Port McNeill to Sointula

The Malcolm Island Ferry takes passengers to the island town of Sointula north of Port McNeill. The town was first settled in 1901 by Finnish immigrants fed up with working in James Dunsmuir's coal mines. When it appeared Dunsmuir would stifle labor organization in his mines, the Finns decided to build a utopian community of their own. They called it *Sointula*, which means "harmony" in Finnish, and, joined by other Finns from Finland and the United States, established a colony on Malcolm Island.

They also invited Matti Kurikka, who had attempted to establish a similar colony in Australia, to come to British Columbia to lead them in their project. Money was always a problem at Sointula, however, and Kurikka turned out to be an inept leader. Despite their efforts toward cooperative socialism, and despite the long hours of farming, fishing and logging, Sointula's grand experiment failed. The colony formally disbanded in 1905. Many of the original members of the community stayed on Malcolm Island, however, and in 1909, they organized the first cooperative store in British Columbia. Today, many of Malcolm Island's residents are descended from Sointula's first settlers, and the Co-op Store is still operating in the community.

Alert Bay Potlatch Busted
Alert Bay Ferry from Port McNeill to Alert Bay on Cormorant Island

In 1922, Alert Bay, east of Port McNeill at the head of Johnstone Strait, was the scene of one of the most notorious of the many repressive acts the Canadian government inflicted on the aboriginal people of the West Coast. After a potlatch ceremony here, the government confiscated a huge quantity of Indian artifacts, particularly potlatch regalia, and jailed prominent Kwakiutl chief Dan Cranmer.

Kwakiutl Indians display 2,000 Hudson's Bay Company blankets during a potlatch.

The potlatch ceremony played a critical role in West Coast Indian culture. According to George Dawson, who made some of the earliest detailed observations of potlatch ceremonies, potlatches often helped unite the tribe in common labor. For instance, a man intending to build a house might hold a potlatch, distributing his material goods among people who would later help build the new house. Other occasions suitable for a potlatch might include the raising of a memorial pole for a deceased chief or the coming of age of a chief's daughter.

The potlatch was highly systematized, so everyone knew ahead of time what would be given to each person. For the most part, the giver could expect to have goods of greater value returned to him in the future, rather like interest on a loan. Holding a potlatch was also a way to build influence. The more frequently and lavishly an individual distributed his property, the more important he became to the rest of the tribe and the more he would be owed when others held potlatches of their own.

The selection of a chief, when hereditary tradition failed, was a matter of public consensus reinforced by the potlatch, with a new chief elected after he distributed more wealth among the people than any of the other candidates. In these cases, the potlatch became a kind of election with each candidate required to surpass the others in giving away their material goods. If the first candidate gave out 10 blankets, the next would try to give out 20. The first would then try to top the second by giving out 25 more, with the process continuing—each candidate being secretly supplied with additional goods by members of the tribe—until a winner emerged. In this way, the winner would be the candidate with the most support in the community.

But when white missionaries arrived on the coast, they viewed the potlatch as pagan extravagance, an integral part of the Indian culture they hoped to replace. Lobbied by missionaries, the federal government amended the Indian Act in 1884 to outlaw potlatches as well as other native feasts and spirit dances. Clandestine potlatches continued to be held in the backwaters of the coast, but native ceremonial life suffered such a debilitating blow that many thought the potlatch was dead. Then, in 1922, the prominent Kwakiutl chief Dan Cranmer defied the law and threw what some say may have been the largest potlatch in history.

Indians came from up and down the coast to take part in the feasts and dancing, and to receive gifts of blankets, food and clothing. The local Indian agent called in the Royal Canadian Mounted Police, and the chiefs were arrested. The government, however, allowed any chief who turned over his potlatch regalia to the Mounties to go free. Many complied and most of the ceremonial material from Cranmer's potlatch was eventually sent to the National Museum in Ottawa—although some of the choicest pieces also went to private collectors in both Canada and the United States. Dan Cranmer refused to accept any bargain with the government, so he was sent to prison.

It wasn't until 1951, after years of almost irreparable damage had been done to Indian culture, that the anti-potlatch law was finally repealed. The ceremonial regalia seized at Alert Bay was never exhibited at the National Museum, but it remained there for over 50 years, locked in storage in the museum basement.

Finally, after long protests, the collection was returned to the Kwakiutl people. Today, some of these ceremonial artifacts can be seen at two local museums dedicated to the preservation of native heritage on the West Coast. One, the U'Mista Cultural Centre, is at Alert Bay, the other at Cape Mudge on Quadra Island.

Fort Rupert Built to Protect Coal
Highway 19, 24 miles (39 km) north of Port McNeill, Centennial Park, Port Hardy

An old stone fireplace and chimney are all that remain of the Fort Rupert Hudson's Bay post. Built in 1849 largely to protect the development of nearby coal deposits, the fort was never a major trading post. Since the coal deposits never amounted to much and were soon abandoned in favor of better coal found farther south, the principle benefit of a post here was to serve Indians who had been left without a trading center on this part of the coast after the closure of Fort McLoughlin at Bella Bella in 1843. The fort also stimulated the growth of a permanent settlement at Port Hardy.

Governor Blanshard Busy at Fort Rupert
Highway 19, 24 miles (39 km) north of Port McNeill, Centennial Park, Port Hardy

Vancouver Island's first colonial governor, Richard Blanshard, arrived in Victoria in March 1850 but had very little to do once he arrived. Blanshard had been in such a hurry to enter government service that he accepted the post of colonial governor even though it came with no salary and very little in the way of prestige. Vancouver Island, at that time, had virtually no independent settlers. There was no civil service. No taxes. No colonial treasury. Even Blanshard's expenses were to be paid from his own pocket. It was the Hudson's Bay Company that exercised the real power in the new colony during Governor Blanshard's brief term in office here.

Not long after Blanshard arrived on Vancouver Island, a miners' strike at Fort Rupert sparked the most significant event

Kwakiutl Indians at Fort Rupert, circa 1946.

of his stay here. Several of the miners decided to run out on their contract with the Hudson's Bay Company and go to California, where a gold rush was still underway. While hiding in the near-by forest and planning their escape to the California gold fields, three of these deserters were killed by Nahwitti Indians during a skirmish north of today's Port Hardy. Finding it necessary to

Abandoned buildings at Fort Rupert.

invoke the Queen's Law against the Indians, Governor Blanshard headed for Fort Rupert aboard the Royal Navy's HMS *Daedalus*.

Nahwitti chief Nancy admitted that the murders had been committed by three of his tribesmen. But when Blanshard and his hastily appointed temporary magistrate Dr. H.M. Helmcken demanded the killers surrender, the Indians refused. The chief offered reparations according to Indian custom, but this did not satisfy Blanshard. He ordered the destruction of the Nahwitti village, which was accomplished without opposition since the Indians had slipped away before the Royal Navy arrived. As a result of their early departure, Blanshard failed to capture the three men who were reportedly responsible for the murders.

In July 1851, however, Blanshard sent the navy back again to a village the Nahwitti had built on an island in Bull Harbour. Again, most of the Indians escaped ahead of time, but once more the village was destroyed. By now the Indians had turned against the three tribesmen wanted by the whites, so when Governor Blanshard offered a reward for their capture, the Indians killed two of them and the slave of the third, and turned the bodies over to the whites. There is no record if Blanshard ever paid out the reward money, but no further action was taken against the Indians for the killing of the three miners.

Last British Columbia Whaling Outfit Ceases Operations
Coal Harbour Road, 10 miles (16 km) southwest of Port Hardy,
Coal Harbour

No British Columbia whaling crews have killed whales along this coast since the Western Canadian Whaling Company, a joint Japanese–Canadian venture operating out of Coal Harbour, ceased harvesting sperm whales in 1967. Whaling on the British Columbia coast before this time dates back to pre-European contact. The Nootka were the only West Coast Indians who hunted whales, although only three Nootka tribes—the Ahousat of Clayoquot Sound, the Moachat of Nootka Sound and the Makah on Cape Flattery—made a regular practice of catching whales.

Whaling for the Nootka had a strong ritual and spiritual side, but the adventure and excitement of the hunt itself was also celebrated. Speared from above with 18' (5.5-m) shell-headed harpoons, the whales would thrash and often jump completely out of the water, trying to shake the lance. After an initial period of frenzied flight, the whale would settle down and a second canoe with another harpooner would attack, setting the whole operation in motion once more. Often the whale would break for the open sea, but eventually, after repeated harpooning, the animal would tire and the men would move in for the agonizing and bloody kill.

When white whalers first arrived on the northwest coast, their methods were no less cruel, but the numbers of whales they sought and killed far exceeded anything the Nootka had ever dreamed. British whalers began hunting on the Pacific coast as early as the 1790s, and New Englanders started around 1810. At the time there was no market for anything but the oil, so after their blubber was stripped and rendered, the whales were left along the coast to rot.

The first true British Columbia whaling industry didn't arrive until 1868, when James Dawson joined forces with San Francisco whaler Abel Douglass to form the Dawson and Douglass Company. Sailing in a schooner named *Kate,* the company began hunting whales off the Saanich Peninsula, killing eight whales in its first season and collecting 2,400 gallons (10,910 l) of oil. The following year Dawson and Douglass moved north to Cortez Island to establish a whaling station at what would become Whaletown. Hunting was good, particularly for humpbacks, although the whales seldom died easily. After three years of intense hunting, however, the whales simply disappeared from the British Columbia coast. The Dawson and Douglass Company abandoned the enterprise.

By the 1890s, whale sightings encouraged others to attempt commercial whaling once more, but none of the enterprises succeeded until about the turn of the century, when whale numbers had increased enough to make hunting profitable once more. Modern technology, in the form of harpoons with exploding heads, killed the whales more quickly and perhaps more humanely. But at the same time, the science of whale killing had progressed to the point that whalers were able to take far more animals and extend their hunt over a much longer period than ever before.

Eventually, however, the whale population on the British Columbia coast was once again decimated by the whalers. The hunt was largely abandoned. Then in the late 1940s, after more than a decade of virtually no whale hunting on the coast, a final whaling outfit was organized. The Western Canadian Whaling Company set up a station at Coal Harbour from an old Royal Canadian Air Force base abandoned at the end of the war. Just as in the past, the company experienced initial successes, which lasted throughout the 1950s. In 1962, the company merged with a Japanese whaling firm, and the combined company enjoyed two more good years. But whale numbers had dropped substantially by 1965, and by 1967, the company was finished. There has been no whaling on the British Columbia coast since.

Last Civil War Casualty Occurs on Vancouver Island
Coal Harbour Road, 10 miles (16 km) southwest of Port Hardy, Coal Harbour

William Clarke Quantrill, an irregular Confederate army officer, operating in Kansas and Missouri during the American Civil War, earned a reputation as the most bloodthirsty fighter in a region infamously known as Bloody Kansas. In this border region between north and south, ordinary citizens were brutally murdered for being sympathetic to one side or the other. Quantrill's reputation as the most ruthless of all was sealed when he led a guerrilla attack on the undefended town of Lawrence,

Kansas, killing over 150 men, women and children in 1864.

The next year a Michigan cavalry troop surrounded and attacked Quantrill and his men, virtually wiping them out. Supposedly, Quantrill was captured and sent to prison, where he soon died. But nearly 40 years later, a lumberman named J.E. Duffey, who had fought with the Michigan volunteers during the Civil War and who knew Quantrill, reported meeting his old Civil War enemy near Quatsino on Vancouver Island. Quantrill, Duffey said, was going by the name John Sharp and had lived in the Coal Harbour area for years. The *Victoria Colonist* ran the story in 1907, and it was soon picked up by other papers throughout the United States.

Not long afterward, two mysterious men came aboard the steamer *Tees* at Victoria and sailed north up the west coast of Vancouver Island to Quatsino. The vessel docked at Quatsino for only a few hours, but the two men arranged for boat transportation to Coal Harbour, where they managed to accomplish whatever business they had to do in time to return to Quatsino before the *Tees* left on its return trip to Victoria. Meanwhile, the dying body of John Sharp, or William Clarke Quantrill, stabbed with a poker, was found in his cabin near Coal Harbour. Warrants were issued for the arrest of the two mysterious strangers. But by the time news of the murder reached Victoria, the *Tees* had already docked, and the two men had left on a Seattle-bound steamer. American authorities were contacted, but by that time the American steamer had already landed in Seattle. No trace of the two men was ever found. Quantrill, or Sharp, became perhaps the final casualty of the American Civil War.

Cape Scott Colonists Settle Holberg
Road to Cape Scott, 30 miles (48 km) west of Port Hardy, Holberg

Today, the northwest corner of Vancouver Island, from Holberg to Queen Charlotte Sound, including all of Cape Scott Provincial Park, is almost uninhabited. Historically, however, its original settlements were so interconnected that it could almost have been said the entire region was a single, sprawling community.

The original settlers on Cape Scott were Danes who founded the Cape Scott Colony in 1897. But the idea for a Danish colony here started three years earlier, when Rasmus Hansen came ashore during a fishing expedition to Queen Charlotte Sound. Hansen liked what he saw of the area, and along with three other Danish immigrants to the United States, he began planning a colony. Eventually, the British Columbia government granted him land along with the promise of a dike to hold back salt water from Goose Harbour. Roads to connect the colony to the outside world were also promised.

As it turned out, the colonists themselves were the only ones to ever build a dike and adequate roads were never built. Even title to the land came under question. Still, the settlers came to the Cape Scott area, settling first near Fisherman's Bay in today's park. By 1899, the settlers had built a dike 2,300' (70 m) long across the lagoon near the mouth of Fisherman River to provide more meadowland for hay and grazing.

After the dike was completed, the community held a celebration that lasted through the night. Outside, as the colonists celebrated, a southeast gale came up, and when the revelers looked toward the bay the next morning, the dike was gone, washed away in the storm. Dismayed but not yet disillusioned, the settlers set to work and built another dike. Completed in 1905, it was farther up the lagoon and constructed at a slight angle to the prevailing winds to protect it from the gales that turned out to be rather common on the cape.

Weather was not the major problem that plagued the settlers at Cape Scott, however. The isolation in which they found themselves turned out to be a bigger stumbling block than it was in most frontier communities of the time, imposing severe limits on what hard work alone could accomplish. The monthly steamer to Cape Scott turned out to be inadequate, especially since there were no docking facilities at Fisherman's Bay. Without roads, access to distant markets for local products never developed sufficiently to support a stable economy.

Eventually, the colonists abandoned the settlement on Cape Scott and most moved farther south to take up 160 homesteads. There, at Quatsino Sound, they felt there was a chance roads might be built and better sea transportation would be available. In this area, especially near today's Holberg in the San Josef Valley to the west and on the sound itself, the Danes mixed with pioneers of other nationalities. The Andersons, Bjerrgaards, Jensens and Glerups were the first of many settlers on the upper

West Arm—on today's Holberg Inlet—and they named the new community Holberg in honor of a famous Danish poet.

Doctor's Advice for Dry Climate Sends Man to British Columbia
12 miles (19 km) west of Holberg, San Josef Bay

Henry Ohlsen at his Cape Scott store in 1905.

The promise of a colony at Cape Scott sparked considerable interest throughout the Danish community in the United States. So when Henry Ohlsen of Dyke, Iowa, learned he had an advanced case of pulmonary tuberculosis, he left immediately for British Columbia. Ohlsen's doctor had told him he might live another six months with his disease, but only if he moved to a place with an exceedingly dry climate. Perhaps the Arizona desert would do the trick.

Instead, Ohlsen took his family and moved to the western edge of Vancouver Island. It was one of the wettest spots in North America, but it was a place where Danes like himself were involved in a grand adventure. Ohlsen homesteaded 160 acres (65 ha) of land a couple of miles inland from the mouth of the San Josef River in 1904. Four years later he opened a small store for settlers who had moved from the Cape Scott Colony to this location, which was closer to an adequate harbor. The San Josef area also seemed more likely to get a road from the eastern side of the island. Although the road was never built, Ohlsen's store was on the main trail between the old Cape Scott Colony and Holberg, and until 1944, Ohlsen lived a vigorous life, raising a family, running the post office and operating the store. He lived, winter after rainy winter, to the ripe old age of 76, forty years longer than the six months the doctor back in Iowa had promised him if he moved to a desert.

Chapter 4

Mountains and Fjords

The Sunshine Coast,
North Coast and Queen
Charlotte Islands

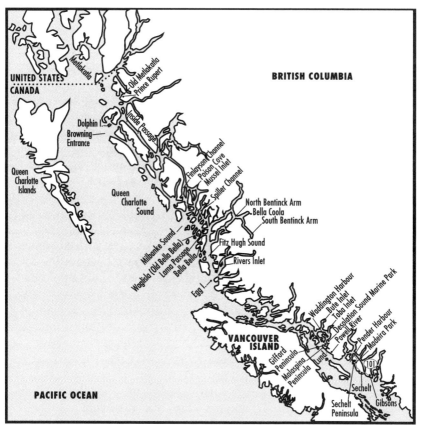

NORTH OF VANCOUVER the British Columbia coast—which forms the most formidable portion of that long-used north–south waterway called the Inside Passage—becomes a continuous series of islands, straits, peninsulas, inlets, wilderness bays and long, narrow channels. Fjords, sometimes with several branches, slice far into the coastal mountains. Everywhere, forests fill the spaces between snow-covered mountain peaks and ocean.

The crossing from Howe Sound on the first leg of the journey north, to today's Sunshine Coast, gives only a hint of both the isolation and sense of community once found along the entire coast above the lower mainland. In the early days there were no roads. Communities were connected to one another and to the outside world by steamers. Until the 1950s, the scheduled arrivals and departures of the steamships were to coastal community life what the railroads were to frontier prairie towns. Food, clothing, tools, mail and visitors all arrived on the coast by steamship. For the people of the north coast, the sea was both a livelihood and the highway, and it gave everyone who lived there a common bond that created a sense of a larger community.

Not so many years ago, logging and fishing communities seemed to lie at the head of every good-sized inlet and harbor. Canneries scattered themselves along the entire coast from Vancouver to Prince Rupert. Gyppo loggers (independent contractors supplying logs to mills) operated along the coast in every nook and cranny where the land offered access to the forests and sea.

Today, places on the coast where people once lived are empty. Like the prairies, most of the north coast is less populated now than it was 40 years ago. Natural harbors where small communities once flourished lie empty or have become homes to small marinas where pleasure boats dock and buy fuel. Dozens of cruise ships ply the waters of the Inside Passage every summer, but the Union steamships, sailing the north coast and sustaining its communities, have, like many of the communities themselves, disappeared.

Automobile traffic is limited on the north coast. In the south, Highway 101, along with two British Columbia ferry connections, link Vancouver and the lower mainland with the Sunshine Coast as far north as Lund. Another car ferry can take vehicles to the rather limited road system of the Queen Charlotte Islands. The

Union steamship vessel at Knight Inlet.

A logging camp near today's Chemainus.

only other coastal communities with road links to the mainland are found at Bella Coola, Kitimat, Prince Rupert and Stewart. The rest of the coast looks, as it always has, to the sea.

For today's visitors, whether traveling by highway or ferry, pleasure or tour boat, it's the isolation of the land along the northwest coast that penetrates deepest into their sensibilities. But the isolation felt is more than geographical. For most visitors, the solitude of the coast takes on spiritual dimensions as well. This is remarkable country, unique in North America because of its separateness as much as its incredibly rugged and beautiful landscape. In some ways the Inside Passage along the British Columbia coast is as imposing for today's travelers as it was for the first explorers and fur traders who sailed its waters 200 years ago. Each long fjord, each rocky bay, each island-dotted channel is a special place where people can pass by, but almost no one can stay.

Gibsons Land at Gibson's Landing
Highway 101, 3 miles (5 km) southwest of Langdale Ferry Landing, Gibsons

Today's popular tourist town of Gibsons, often called by its original name of Gibson's Landing, was the filming site for the television series *The Beachcombers* in the 1980s. A hundred years earlier, in the 1880s, Gibsons was unsettled country. But in 1886, George Gibson and his sons Ralph and George Jr. set off from Nanaimo in their handmade sloop, the *Swamp Angel*, looking for a suitable place to homestead. The Gibsons first looked at land at Oyster Bay near Ladysmith on Vancouver Island. Not finding anything to their liking there they set out across the Strait of Georgia, bound for Vancouver.

As they traveled, however, a storm with a strong southeast wind blew the trio off course and across the entrance of Howe Sound, where they took shelter on Keats Island, opposite today's Gibsons. Anchoring for the night in a quiet, natural harbor on the south side of the island, the three men waited until the following morning for the wind to die down. Before heading back to sea, however, the Gibsons crossed Shoal Channel to a nearby headland. Here they found the site so appealing that they decided to each file a claim for 160 acres (65 ha) of it. Later

The Inside Passage.

that summer, other Gibson family members arrived. The following year a married daughter, Mary Glassford, came with her husband and family. Other settlers followed and a community grew near where the Gibsons had happened to land that summer day in 1886, blown off course in a storm but eventually finding their way to a place that would become known as Gibson's Landing.

Fjords Cut by Glaciers
Highway 101, 16 miles (26 km) north of Langdale Ferry Landing, Sechelt Peninsula, Sechelt

The rugged fjords of the British Columbia coast were carved by Pleistocene glaciers about a million years ago. These glaciers were created from the accumulation of snow built up year after year in the coastal mountains. Eventually, the glaciers grew so heavy that their immense weight began pushing them down the mountains, carving steep canyons as they went. As similar glaciers around the world grew larger, the level of the oceans dropped and exposed huge areas of today's coast. For thousands of years, the mountains stood far from the sea. But as the glaciers melted and the oceans rose, the sea came to the mountains. Canyons and riverbeds were taken over by the ocean, forming narrow channels and inlets, like those that created the Sechelt Peninsula, all along the British Columbia coast from Burrard Inlet to the Alaskan Panhandle.

Sechelt Establish First Independent Aboriginal Government in Canada
Highway 101, 16 miles (26 km) north of Langdale Ferry Landing, Sechelt Peninsula, Sechelt

Much of the land on the south side of the town of Sechelt belongs to the Sechelt People, a coastal Salish tribe who lived on the Sechelt Peninsula for countless generations before the first Europeans arrived 200 years ago. Before white contact, the Sechelt population stood somewhere between 5,000 and 15,000. Just as in other native communities across the continent, however, the arrival of Europeans and their diseases meant illness and death for many Sechelt. By the 1860s, after a final devastating smallpox epidemic, their numbers had fallen to only a few hundred.

At the same time the Sechelt were being devastated by smallpox and other diseases, the Indians were proselytized by European missionaries of the Oblate Order led by Father Paul Durieu. Like other missionaries on the coast, Durieu made it clear to the Sechelt that the only way to protect themselves from smallpox and other European diseases was to follow his Christian teachings. In 1868, he built a central mission at today's town of Sechelt, where for the next 30 years the Oblates ruled with something close to brutality. Everyone was compelled to rise with the ringing of the church bell in the morning and go to bed with the ringing of the bell at night. The penalty for missing church, which was held twice each day, was 40 lashes.

While the Oblates ministered to the Indians, stripping them of virtually every vestige of their original culture, the government set about taking the Indians' land. In eastern Canada each native family was allowed to keep 80 acres (32 ha) and in parts of Western Canada, 160 acres (65 ha). But in the Colony of British Columbia, Governor Douglas began the task of liquidating native claims by demanding that aboriginal people keep no more than 10 acres (4 ha). At Sechelt, not even 1 acre (.4 ha) per person was set aside for the Indians around the Oblate mission.

Sechelt Indians, circa 1890.

In 1871, when British Columbia became a province in the newly formed Canada, the Sechelt land was turned over to the federal government along with the other land reserves for native people in British Columbia. Almost immediately, the new province passed a law outlawing native people from preempting land for themselves under the homesteading laws of the time. White settlers could claim 160 acres (65 ha) almost anywhere in the province, but native people were barred from the process even though their claims to the land were far from extinguished.

As white settlers began taking up land around them, the Sechelt complained to the government about the injustice. In 1874, the Moodyville Sawmill Company began cutting timber on what Chief Schelle considered Indian territory. The Indians complained, but nothing was done, although the company did agree to buy logs from the Indians so long as they were cut from timber standing on the reserve itself. In 1875, Chief Schelle went to the editor of the *Mainland Guardian* in New Westminster in an attempt to get the newspaper to publicize their grievances. The paper published an editorial decrying the fate of the Sechelt people, but it took more than a year before the government added another 600 acres (243 ha) to the Sechelt Reserve. That still only gave the Sechelt about 4 acres (1.6 ha) per person.

Over the years the band at Sechelt acquired additional land bit by bit, never backing down on their claims even during the years between 1924 and 1951, when the federal government enforced a law forbidding any formal Indian land claim without the written consent of the Department of Indian Affairs. Today, the Sechelt Reserve includes more than 2,000 acres (809 ha) with additional land claims still to be settled. In 1986, the governments of Canada, British Columbia and the Sechelt people signed an agreement bringing about the Sechelt Indian District Government, which works within the existing federal and provincial framework. The agreement replaced the federal government's Indian Act with laws and a constitution of the Sechelt people themselves, and it established the first independent aboriginal government in Canada.

Bert Whitaker Builds Fortune Watering Milk
Highway 101, 16 miles (26 km) north of Langdale Ferry Landing, Sechelt Peninsula, Sechelt

One of Sechelt's earliest entrepreneurs, Bert Whitaker, came to the area in 1892, when he was just 17 years old. Almost immediately, he embarked on a series of money-making ventures. Whitaker and his father each preempted 160 acres (65 ha) of land on Porpoise Bay and began logging. In 1895, Whitaker bought more land, giving him almost 2 miles (3.2 km) of waterfront on Trail and Porpoise bays. After buying his land on Trail Bay, Whitaker opened a store, and in early 1896, became the first postmaster in Sechelt. Two years later he built a larger store, and the year after that he opened a hotel. Early in the new century, Whitaker built rental cottages west of his hotel for vacationers. Two of these (Rock Cottage next to Snickett Park and Green Cottage a block to the east) are still standing.

Despite being the area's leading businessman, Bert Whitaker also developed a penny-pinching reputation. His wharf on Porpoise Bay was allowed to fall into such disrepair that it collapsed in 1959, finally necessitating the construction of the new wharf. Loggers who came to Sechelt from Jervis Inlet in the early days to catch steamships to Vancouver used to say that when Whitaker's hotel wasn't full he would fake a breakdown on his Porpoise Bay launch so that the loggers would miss their connection to Vancouver and have to spend the night at his hotel. Others recalled that even the milk in Whitaker's general store was secretly watered. When Whitaker died in 1925 at the age of 50, his various businesses were bought out by a branch of the Union Steamship Company.

Pender Harbour Venice of British Columbia Coast
Highway 101, 20 miles (32 km) north of Sechelt, Madeira Park

North Island Princess *on the Powell River, Texada Island Ferry.*

Promoters once called Pender Harbour the Venice of the British Columbia coast. Unlike many communities in the sheltered spots on the coast, Pender Harbour's intricate pattern of bays and islands discouraged the development of a single, large settlement. Instead of one village on the harbor, there were several small landings. Trails along the shore were few because when residents on Pender Harbour went places—whether to visit friends, go to the store or travel to the outside world—they went by boat.

Irvine's Landing—with store, wharf, and hotel—was operating on the north shore at the entrance of the harbor by the 1890s. In 1904, Joe Gonsalves, from the Portuguese Madeira Islands, bought the property. Along with his son-in-law Theodore Dames, Gonsalves then built a larger hotel and saloon. Local fishermen and loggers became customers along with tourists who had been visiting the area since the 1890s. Fishermen and farmers lived across the harbor on the Francis Peninsula in an area that became known as Hardscratch. A store was built at Donley's Landing, a machine shop and boat repair business was set up on Dusenbury Island and for a while a cannery operated at Pender Harbour. By the 1920s, summer homes were being built on the harbor near Garden Bay.

For half a century, though, the families and communities of Pender Harbour depended almost solely on the sea for transportation. All along the harbor, homes faced the water. There was almost no settlement away from the shore. The first road was built in the 1930s, but it wasn't until the 1950s that a paved road connected Sunshine Coast communities from Gibsons to Powell River and the residents of Pender Harbour could truly turn to the land for transportation. Once the road came, people bought cars. Instead of taking a boat, they drove to the store. The kids went to school on the bus. Neighbors living five minutes away by boat visited each other by car, even though it often took twice as long to travel that way. And eventually, the comparisons to Venice stopped.

Paper from First Mill in Western Canada Comes from East

Highway 101, 33 miles (53 km) and a ferry ride north of Madeira Park, Powell River

---

The Minnesota firm of Brooks and Scanlon started the Powell River Paper Company in 1909 and began building the first paper mill in Western Canada at Powell River the following year. Work on the mill was plagued with a number of unforeseen problems, however, and construction was delayed several times. The $1 million raised for the project wasn't enough. Damming the river proved to be a more formidable task than initially anticipated. At one point a cement canal gave way, and river water flooded into the new machine shop being constructed below. Squatters, including a logging railroad, also slowed down construction.

In 1911, when it became obvious that the Powell River Paper Company wasn't going to be able to meet its paper contracts, the company went further into debt and bought huge quantities of paper from eastern mills. For a time Powell River supplied its

*Powell River construction workers taking a break while building
a dam in 1911.*

customers in the west with paper it had bought at higher prices
in the east. Finally, on April 12, 1912, the first roll of paper actually produced in Powell River was hauled to the dock to be shipped
to a customer.

Largest Floating Breakwater in the World

Highway 101, 33 miles (53 km) and a ferry ride north of Madeira Park, Powell River

Powell River paper mill, 1914.

What may be the largest floating breakwater in the world lies at the head of the mill log pond at Powell River. Located on the harbor below Old Town, the only mill town still in existence on the British Columbia coast, the floating breakwater is made up of 10 stripped-down surplus ships. Most of the hulks were built during World War II, and nine of them are constructed of poured concrete. Some are freighters, some oil barges. One was a passenger steamer that used to dock at Powell River. Another ship, the *Peralta,* was built in 1916 and operated as a sardine factory off the coast of Alaska.

The ships are held in place by as many as 10 concrete anchors weighing up to 18,000 pounds (8,165 kg) each. Bridle chains also tie the ships together. The constant pounding of southeast winds, however, pushes the ships closer to shore all the time, and every half dozen years or so the ships have to be repositioned. Periodic repositioning, maintenance and repairs are expensive, but the cost is still small compared to the millions of dollars required to construct a standard breakwater the same length in the harbor's 60–200' (18–61 m) of water.

Billy Goat Smith Buries Treasure and Looks to the Stars
Cranberry Cemetery, Highway 101, 33 miles (53 km) and a ferry ride north of Madeira Park, Powell River

Robert Bonner "Billy Goat" Smith with friends near Powell River.

The hermit Robert Bonner Smith became something of a legend on the British Columbia coast during the first half of the twentieth century. Known as Billy Goat Smith because of the small herd of goats he kept, Smith lived in a small cabin on a 160-acre (65-ha) homestead 30 miles (48 km) from Powell River at the head of Powell Lake. He first came to the British Columbia coast in 1910 after jumping ship in Portland, Oregon, and deserting the U.S. navy.

No one knew why Smith abandoned his navy career, but it was generally believed that his fear of capture by American authorities—which continued long after common sense would dictate—was far out of proportion to his supposed crime. Many suggested that Smith's flight from the U.S. had to do with something more sinister than giving up the navy, but if that were the case, Smith never spoke of it. During World War I, Smith joined the Canadian army and served on the home front before returning to his cabin on Powell Lake immediately after the war. For the next 40 years he never left the area.

Smith peppered his language with words he learned from a

tattered copy of a Webster's dictionary, and he was reported to have had one of the loveliest flower gardens in British Columbia. Smith was also fascinated by the stars, and used to keep a telescope on his front porch. The telescope also allowed Smith to spy on visitors coming up the mountainside from the lake. Since he was known to be one of the best marksmen on the coast, many first-time visitors mistook the telescope for a rifle.

In his younger years Smith sometimes sustained himself by selling timber from his property. Since he was not known to be a spendthrift, the rumor developed that he had a small fortune buried somewhere on his property. In his later years Smith gave up smoking and drinking, and often talked about the stars he watched through his telescope, telling visitors that he planned to go to the stars when he died. In his old age, when people suggested he move to town where he could be cared for, Smith would tell them the only direction he ever planned to travel was up. He died in 1958. His body was found lying in a wheel barrel, looking up at the stars.

Smith was buried in Powell River's Cranberry Cemetery. After his funeral, before the Royal Canadian Mounted Police could return to his cabin, his property was ransacked by someone looking for his supposed buried fortune. No one was ever apprehended for the crime, so it was never known if the rumored fortune was a reality. The police, however, found a jar buried under Smith's fruit cellar that contained $1,800.

Road Ends at Lund
Highway 101, Lund

After 100 miles (161 km) of winding coastal roads with two half-hour ferry rides, the traveler from Vancouver finally reaches the end of the road at Lund. Here, a sign describes the spot not as the end of the road, but the beginning—which, from a local perspective, it is.

Lund was out of the way even before the building of Highway 101 put it at the end of the road. It was founded by a Swedish immigrant, Frederick Gottfrid Thulin, who came to Canada because he heard that workers here didn't have to work in the rain. Thulin arrived in 1890 and called the spot *Lund,* a Swedish word meaning "a grove of trees." The harbor had been used for

Lund Waterfront Hotel, 1912. It was built by the Thulin brothers.

hundreds of years by members of the Salish Indians, who maintained winter homes here. Thulin and his brother logged in the area, built a wharf and store here, and after the Union Steamship Company began making regular stops at Lund, built a hotel in 1894. In the basement, Thulin built a jail, where troublemakers could be locked up overnight. Thulin's hotel, with an excellent restaurant, is still in use, although the jail is not. The road south to Vancouver starts just outside the hotel, but travelers heading north must turn to the sea or air for their transportation.

Unlikely Beauty in Desolation Sound
Along the Inside Passage north of Lund, Malispina and Gifford Peninsula, Desolation Sound Marine Park

Despite its fearful name, Desolation Sound is as beautiful as anywhere on the west coast. In 1792, however, when Captain Vancouver sailed his ship *Discovery* past Sarah Point into the sound, he thought the place gloomy, empty and foreboding. The *Discovery*, along with its sister ship *Chatham* and Galiano's two

Spanish vessels *Sutil* and *Mexicana,* lay at anchor in the sound for several days while he and his men scouted the area in smaller boats.

"Our residence here was truly forlorn," Vancouver wrote in his journal. He continued:

> An awful silence pervaded the gloomy forests, whilst animated nature seemed to have deserted the neighboring country, whose soil afforded only a few small onions, some samphire and here and there more favorable to our wants, the steep rocky shores prevented the use of the seine, and not a fish at the bottom could be tempted to the hook. . . . [the region] afforded not a single prospect that was pleasing to the eye, the smallest recreation on shore, no animal nor vegetable food, excepting a very scanty proportion of those eatables already described, and of which the adjacent country was soon exhausted, after our arrival . . . whence the place obtained the name of Desolation Sound; where our time would have passed infinitely more heavily, had it not been relieved by the agreeable society of our Spanish friends.

Mysterious Table Leads to Toba Inlet
Inside Passage, Toba Inlet

The name Toba Inlet is an accident of history. The inlet was first discovered by the Spanish explorers Valdes and Galiano during their exploration of the northwest coast with Vancouver in 1792. Galiano named it for a mysterious cedar-plank table he found here that was apparently abandoned. The table was covered with Indian hieroglyphics that Galiano found indecipherable.

Unfortunately, Galiano's writing, in turn, was found indecipherable by an early Spanish chart engraver. Galiano had called the inlet the *Canal de la Tabla* in his journals, using the Spanish word for "table," but the map engraver read it as *Canal de la Toba* and noted it as such. Since then the error has been perpetuated on maps. The strange table with the mysterious writing that Galiano reported finding was never seen again by Europeans.

Building Road Leads to Chilcotin War
Inside Passage, Bute Inlet, Waddington Harbour

In the early 1860s, at the height of the Cariboo Gold Rush, the colonial government built the Cariboo Road from New Westminster through the Fraser Canyon to Quesnel. The road diverted business away from Victoria in favor of New Westminster and soon led to a call by Victoria businessmen for a new, shorter route to the gold fields. Build a road from the head of Bute Inlet, they said, or from Bella Coola to the inland. Either of these routes, they claimed, would be a shorter and easier way to the Cariboo. Not coincidentally, of course, it would also divert traffic from the lower mainland back to the shipping port of Victoria.

One Victoria merchant, Alfred Waddington, began promoting the idea of a road from the head of Bute Inlet. Waddington's road would follow the Homathko River to its headwaters, cut cross-country to the Chilcotin River, then followed it to the Fraser River before joining the existing road to Quesnel. Waddington actually started work on his project in 1862, but he lacked the money to make much of the undertaking until the spring of 1864, when, with increased financing from other Victoria merchants, he sent two work crews into the Homathko and Chilcotin country.

Much of the terrain over which Waddington planned to build his road was so rugged that the whole venture should have been in doubt from the beginning. For many Chilcotin Indians, though, who now saw whites intruding on their land from the west as well as the south and east, even this feeble attempt at a road was threatening. Historians have put forward many reasons to explain the uprising that came to be called the Chilcotin War—including mistreatment of the Chilcotins hired to work on the road—but the underlying cause was the familiar one of white occupation of Indian lands without proper regard for the native people involved.

The short-lived war started when a band of Chilcotins attacked and killed ferryman Tim Smith on the Homathko River just downstream from Waddington's work crews. Early the next morning, before the workmen had come out of their tents, the band struck again. Shooting through the canvas tents, the Indians killed all but three of Waddington's men. Farther upstream, at the last camp, four other workers were gunned down, bringing the total dead to 14.

From here the Chilcotin, led primarily by Chief Klatsassin, struck across the Chilcotin plains, killing the only settler in the area, William Manning, who had been homesteading near Puntzi Lake. Not long afterward, the Indians came across a band of horses being driven over the mountains to the gold fields by eight drovers. They killed three of them and chased the other five back over the mountains toward Bella Coola.

When news of the killings reached New Westminster, Governor Seymour sent a force under Police Inspector Charles Brew to put down the rebellion. In the Cariboo, Gold Commissioner William Cox also raised a posse to pursue the Indians from the east. For several weeks Klatsassin and his warriors were chased and harassed throughout the region. Meanwhile, other Chilcotins who hadn't been involved in the rebellion but were suspected of giving aid to Klatsassin were pressured to stay out of the conflict and turn against the Indians who were involved. On August 15, Klatsassin and seven of his warriors were persuaded to give themselves up, partly because Cox extended a promise of amnesty.

Governor Seymour realized that pursuit of the other members of the insurrection was pointless because it would be almost impossible to track them down in their own country. As a result, even though Klatsassin maintained that at least 10 others had been directly involved in the killings, Seymour chose to put the warriors he had on trial and not worry about the rest. Five of the Indians, including Klatsassin, were found guilty and then hanged at Quesnel. Other Indians who were involved in the rebellion stayed out of sight for a time, but they eventually returned home to their communities when it became evident that the whites were satisfied with their revenge.

Lighthouse Keeper Commits Suicide
Inside Passage, Egg Island, Queen Charlotte Sound

The Egg Island Light Station, perched on a rocky island on the eastern edge of Queen Charlotte Sound since 1898, has seemed a bleak and isolated posting for many of its keepers. Several times storms have blown the open waters of the sound across the island with enough force to destroy the station. At least two keepers have disappeared without a trace over the years, and one, Laurie Dupris, committed suicide.

Dupris had come to the island with his new wife, Peggy, and her son, Stanley, from a previous marriage. Isolated on Egg Island, however, tensions began to grow between the couple as their first winter passed. In the spring Peggy took her son on a trip to Vancouver, and while they were gone a telegram arrived for Stanley from Peggy's former husband. In his depressed state, Dupris interpreted the telegram to mean his wife was leaving him to return to her former husband. In despair, Dupuis shot himself, leaving a note telling Peggy that he'd rather die than live without her.

Owikeno Massacred by Bella Bella
Inside Passage, Rivers Inlet

The Owikeno people living at Owikeno village at the head of Rivers Inlet tell a legend about a time when many of their tribe were massacred by the Bella Bella, their more powerful relatives farther up the coast. It happened about 1848, after the Bella Bella, in a trick to obtain additional slaves, invited the Owikeno people to a potlatch at Kwakwame Bay. When the Owikeno arrived at the potlatch, however, they found the Bella Bella waiting in ambush. Almost all of the Owikeno men were killed, and the Owikeno women and children were taken for slaves. Only the people in two canoes escaped to return to Rivers Inlet.

Even here, however, the reduced population of Owikeno people was unsafe. The following day the Bella Bella surprised them again when they attacked the principal Owikeno village, Katil, on Lake Owikeno, upstream on the Wannock River from the head of Rivers Inlet. In the second raid, three more Owikeno men and one woman were killed, and thirty-two more women and children were enslaved.

Suspected Murderer Disappears
Inside Passage, Addenbroke Island Lighthouse, Addenbroke Island, Fitz Hugh Sound

Ernie Maynard took over the Addenbroke Lighthouse in the spring of 1928, but his stay at the post was short-lived. In August of his first summer on the job, someone shot Maynard in the face and left him to die at the lonely light station. Once his body was found, provincial police searched the area but discovered no clues about the identity of the murderer. Their only suspect was a beachcomber named Manuel Hannah, who often camped on nearby Calvert Island.

Hannah had a prison record, and a provincial police constable returned to Calvert Island several times to interrogate him about the murder. Over and over, Hannah insisted that he had no knowledge of the killing, but the provincial police kept at him. Then one day later in the summer, Hannah suddenly disappeared. On their last visit to Calvert Island to question the ex-con, police found only a note denying once more that Hannah had anything to do with the murder and telling them not to bother looking for him. He would be in "a better land" by the time they received the note. It's not known if Hannah committed suicide or left the country, but no trace of the suspected murderer was ever found.

Alexander Mackenzie Beats Lewis and Clark Across the Continent
Inside Passage, North Bentinck Arm, Bella Coola

Alexander Mackenzie crossed North America from the east to reach the Pacific Ocean here on July 22, 1793—the first European to complete such a journey north of Mexico. Mackenzie arrived on the northwest coast more than 10 years before Lewis and Clark made a similar crossing of the American West.

Mackenzie had hoped to find an economical route for shipping furs from Canada's subarctic interior to the Pacific. His amazing journey took him up the Peace River, where he wintered near the present-day Alberta community of that name. Then in the spring, he followed the Peace River over the mountain divide and traveled part way down the Fraser River. Informed by Indians that that river would soon become unnavigable, Mackenzie left the Fraser to travel cross-country, following an Indian trade route over the coastal mountains to the Pacific near present-day Bella Coola. Coincidentally, Captain George Vancouver had explored North Bentinck Arm while mapping the northwest coast only a few weeks before Mackenzie arrived.

The first school class at Bella Coola.

Mackenzie stayed in the Bella Coola area only a couple of days, traveling as far as Cascade Inlet, where, on the southeast face of a large rock, he inscribed the famous words, "Alexander Mackenzie from Canada by land, the twenty-second day of July, one thousand seven hundred and ninety-three." Because of the general hostility of the coastal Indians in the region beyond Bella Coola, Mackenzie returned almost immediately to the Peace River district.

Wrong Name Becomes Three Bella Bella
Inside Passage, Old Bella Bella, Waglisla and Bella Bella; Lama Passage

When the Hudson's Bay Company built Fort McLoughlin on Campbell Island in 1833, Indians from nearby communities settled close to the fort. Traders, for reasons now unclear, began calling the people of the new village, and the village itself, Bella Bella—even though the people called themselves, then and now, Heiltsuk. Some suggest that the name Bella Bella referred to a point of land south of the community, but for whatever reason, the name Bella Bella persisted for both people and place.

In 1842, the Hudson's Bay Company abandoned Fort McLoughlin after building Fort Victoria. A few years later, in

1849, when Fort Rupert on the north end of Vancouver Island was built near today's Port Hardy, most of the Indians at Bella Bella moved to that community. It looked as if Bella Bella might eventually be abandoned altogether, but by the latter part of the nineteenth century, the old settlement had grown again, following the immigration of Indians to the community from other coastal settlements. The town had grown so large, in fact, that most of the 300 people decided to move to a larger site. A new Bella Bella was built a couple of miles north of the old town around the turn of the century. Today, it is known as Waglisla.

Meanwhile, early in the twentieth century, a cannery was built across Lama Passage from Bella Bella's Campbell Island site and a new settlement developed that was generally referred to as East Bella Bella. But as both previous Bella Bella began to be referred to as Old Town and Waglisla, it became simply Bella Bella.

Bella Bella Make Steamship
Inside Passage, Old Bella Bella, Waglisla and Bella Bella; Lama Passage

---

The SS Beaver *in Victoria Harbour, 1870.*

When traders first arrived at Fort McLoughlin, there were several local bands in the area. One band, the Bella Bella, or Heiltsuk, was particularly impressed with the Hudson's Bay Company steamer *Beaver.* The *Beaver* was the only steamship on the coast, and it seemed to capture the imagination of local Indians wherever it went. The Heiltsuk told company officers that they, too, would acquire a steamship. And they did, in a manner of speaking.

The Heiltsuk boat was a scaled-down version of the real *Beaver.* The Indians built it from one large, hollowed-out cedar tree trunk. A third the length of the *Beaver's* 100' (31 m), the Heiltsuk steamer was painted black, with painted ports, a wooden deck and red paddle wheels powered by the exertions of Indians hidden below deck. The *Beaver II* was a remarkably close copy of the real *Beaver* in appearance, and it could travel about 3 miles (5 km) per hour, pretty good considering the real *Beaver's* steam-powered maximum speed was only 9 miles (14.5 km) per hour.

American Ship Narrowly Escapes Indians
Inside Passage, Sturgis Bay, Spiller Channel

Just north of today's Bella Bella at Spiller Channel, an American trading ship, the *Atahualta,* was attacked and nearly captured by Chief Kaiete and his band of Bella Bella Indians in the early summer of 1805. Most of the crew were wounded and nearly half were killed, including the captain, second mate, cook and seven others. Neither written records nor Indian accounts handed down over the years tell why the ship was attacked. In fact, only the week before the *Atahualta* sailed into Spiller Channel, another Boston trading vessel, Captain John Sturgis's *Caroline,* had stopped at the little bay that now bares Sturgis's name. Sturgis had had no trouble dealing with the Indians during his short stay and saw no signs of trouble brewing. A few days later, when the *Atahualta* sailed into Sturgis Bay, everything was different.

Indian and white accounts of what took place are in almost total agreement. Chief Kaiete and a number of band members boarded the ship, ostensibly for purposes of trade. Kaiete asked Captain Porter to look at a large canoe filled with furs. When the captain bent over the rail to have a look, Kaiete flung a blanket over his head and repeatedly stabbed him with a knife. When Captain Porter stopped struggling, Kaiete threw the body overboard.

By this time other Indians were boarding the ship and a full-scale battle was underway. The ship's cook, John Williams, came out throwing pots of boiling water on the Indians, water that left several of them blind for the rest of their lives and caused others to lose their hair. When Williams ran out of hot water, one of the Bella Bella killed him with an ax. Only four of the crew members remained alive and unhurt. They managed to get below deck where the crew kept a store of loaded muskets. Returning to the deck, they drove the Indians into the sea.

Once the decks were cleared, the sailors raised sail and headed for open sea. Of the 200 Indians who were said to have been involved in the attack as many as 40 may have lost their lives. The next day, the surviving crew members buried 10 of their comrades at sea.

Poison Clams Kill Seaman
Inside Passage, Mussel Inlet, Finlayson Channel, Milbanke Sound; Poison Cove

---

The ominous name for Poison Cove resulted from an incident here in 1793, when crew members of Captain Vancouver's ship *Discovery* stopped to gather mussels. The mussels were roasted for breakfast, and within an hour of eating them, sailors began getting sick to their stomachs. Many felt a general numbness. Officers advised the men to stop and drink hot salt water to induce vomiting, but the men declined on the grounds that the illness wasn't that serious.

A few hours later, however, one of the men, seaman John Carter, still working the oars, suddenly became too weak to row. A stop was made at today's Carter Bay, southwest of Poison Cove on Finlayson Channel, but Carter soon died in spite of any assistance his fellows could render. At this point the other men quickly heated salt water and began drinking it. That brought on the desired effect, and no other members of the crew died from the poisoned mussels.

Legend Created Surrounding First Visit to Coast
Inside Passage, Dolphin Island, Browning Entrance; Kitkatla

No one knows when the first Europeans came to this part of the coast, but the Kitkatla people have passed on an oral account that might offer some clues. The legend was first told to the famous missionary William Duncan at Metlakatla in 1860. According to the story, a party of Indians was fishing near here when they heard what they thought might be a sea monster. The Indians immediately headed for shore, where they abandoned their canoes and hid in the trees.

The monster proved to be a large boat with "sticks" that were raised all at once so that "water dropped from them like tears." Strange men got out of the boat and came ashore, where one of the men made an instantaneous flash of fire from his hand that started a fire to cook their food. The Indians, who had no metal cooking utensils at the time, were also amazed to see a

Haida Medicine Man, Queen Charlotte Islands.

pot that didn't burn when it was put into the flames. They were also surprised at the food—probably rice—which looked like maggots.

Another amazing feat occurred when a man pointed what appeared to be a piece of wood at a goose flying overhead. The wooden stick made a flash of fire and a loud, horrid sound, and the goose fell out of the sky. Most amazing of all, after the fog cleared, a monster canoe with trees growing out of it appeared at sea. The men got into the boat with the long sticks, rowed out to the big canoe, climbed aboard and sailed away.

No record exists of who the white visitors might have been. Duncan did not know if the storyteller had witnessed the scene or was repeating a story. Judging the man's age to be well over 60, Duncan reasoned that if the man had seen the landing personally, the date could have been as early as 1790, when Spanish, British, American and Russian traders could all have been sailing in the region.

Prince Rupert Blows Up During Construction
Inside Passage, Kaien Island, Prince Rupert

The city of Prince Rupert was created after the Grand Trunk Pacific Railway announced that its western terminus would be on Kaien Island. Initial construction of the new city began in May 1906, two years before the railroad would get around to laying out streets and marking lots. By the time the railroad began surveying the new town, Prince Rupert already had 50 businesses and 1,000 residents. Once lots started selling, real estate prices climbed with the kind of speed that usually accompanied major railroad towns during a construction boom.

On Kaien Island's rugged terrain, however, construction often meant blasting rock to prepare sites. Often, entire hillsides would be dynamited away to make acceptable road grades. Ditches had to be blasted open for sewers. More blasting was done to level land for the Grand Trunk Pacific rail yards in the downtown area. So much blasting went on in Prince Rupert's early years, in fact, that accidents and miscalculated explosions of one sort or another seemed an almost daily occurrence.

An early blacksmith shop exploded when a spark from the forge drifted across the shop to land on the pile of dynamite stored carelessly with caps on in the corner. The resulting blast left only a hole in the ground where the blacksmith shop had stood and also completely demolished a hotel next door. Over 1,000 nearby windows were broken.

A patron of another hotel was eating supper one evening when an explosion sent rocks sailing through the hotel's front

Early Prince Rupert.

window, several of which landed on his tin plate. By that time, however, explosions had become such a common occurrence that the diner merely looked up and said to the waitress that he asked her for more bread, not rocks.

Drunk Mistaken for Dead
Centre Street, Prince Rupert

Most of Prince Rupert is built over rugged terrain, but the original Centre Street, the city's first road, was steep even by Prince Rupert standards. Frank Hart was the town undertaker in the early years, and one night he sent his helper up the street carrying a recently deceased client to his funeral parlor, which also served as a local furniture store. On his way up the hill, however, the workman tripped in the dark and the corpse went rolling back down the hill.

The workman groped around in the dark until he found what he thought was the body, picked it up and carried it the rest of the way to the funeral parlor. When Hart went to work on the body, however, he found that the man was still alive but in a drunken stupor. The workman was called back. The story was pieced together, the drunk thrown out on the street again, and Hart and his helper went back to Centre Street with a lantern.

Eventually, they found the real corpse lying in a ditch along the road where it had fallen.

Fort Simpson Namesake Plants First Apple Trees on Pacific Coast
Prince Rupert

Port Simpson, circa 1850.

Fort Simpson, a trading post built just south of today's Prince Rupert on Kaien Island in July 1834, was named for Emilius Simpson, captain of the Hudson's Bay Company's trading vessel *Dryad*. In 1830, Simpson established a trading post at a place on the Nass River known today as Fort Point. He called his new post Fort Nass, but the name was changed to Fort Simpson a few months later when Captain Simpson took sick and died on a voyage to the Queen Charlotte Islands. Three years afterward a new Fort Simpson was built because Hudson's Bay Company officials believed trade would be more profitable on the coast than at the original site. There were about 25 Indian settlements in the area at the time the new Fort Simpson was built. Some were perhaps 4,000 years old, but most of the Indian people abandoned their original homes and moved to new settlements that grew up surrounding the fort.

In addition to having a fort named after him, Emilius Simpson is also known as the man who grew the first apple trees on the northwest coast. According to the story, Simpson was at a going away party the night before he left London for his voyage to North America. At the party a lady friend gave him several apple seeds with instructions to plant them once he arrived in America. Simpson put the seeds in his jacket pocket, where he forgot about them for several months before wearing the jacket again while at Fort Vancouver in today's Washington State. Remembering his promise to his friend, he planted the seeds near the fort and most of them grew into trees.

Metlakatla Moves to Alaska
Inside Passage, Metlakatla Channel, Venn Passage; Metlakatla

William Duncan came to Fort Simpson in 1858 as a lay missionary with the Anglican Church. His instructions had been to work with the 2,000 or so Tsimshian living in the area around the fort. Duncan learned the Tsimshian language and worked for some time among the native people. He then decided in 1862 to lead a band of his Indian followers across what is known today as Prince Rupert Harbour to Metlakatla, a long-settled Tsimshian village that had been largely abandoned since the construction of Fort Simpson. At Metlakatla, Duncan decreed that they would establish a model Christian community, free from the excesses of both white and Indian society.

Duncan's status among the Indians rose precipitously soon after Metlakatla's founding. A smallpox outbreak swept through native communities all along the coast at that time, but the epidemic virtually skipped Duncan's settlement, probably due to its initial isolation and Duncan's decree that his parishioners were to be variolated, a primitive inoculation that used dried scabs from smallpox victims to inoculate the healthy. A few fell sick and died from this procedure, but more than 90 percent developed an immunity to the disease. When the Tsimshian looked at how the disease had ravaged entire communities up and down the coast, they took their good fortune to be proof of Duncan's spiritual power. For a number of years thereafter, Duncan's settlement at Metlakatla was the most successful, at least in white terms, of all the missionary postings along the British Columbia coast.

Metlakatla, circa 1880.

Metlakatla's 1,000 or so residents lived in identical cottages, each with fenced yards and well-tended gardens. A school and church were built. A sawmill provided the community with lumber and men with jobs. A cooperative store opened, and the community became almost self-sufficient as a managed, local economy developed under Duncan's guidance. A police force, a community orchestra and several athletic teams were established. All important aspects of the former Tsimshian culture were, of course, banned.

William Duncan's Christian community was looked on with pride by Anglicans from around the world. Several Anglican officials visited the area, and reports of the industrious, model community were carried back to Europe, where its successes were hailed as miracles and used to raise funds for additional missionary activity along the coast. William Duncan became something of a hero in missionary circles, but he also was something of a dictator at home. Duncan took to authority naturally and resisted compromise or any encroachment on his power. Church officials had no problem with this, of course, just so long as it applied only to Duncan's Indian charges.

It was only a matter of time before conflicts arose between the British Columbia missionary and church authorities. The point of contention that finally split Duncan and Anglican officials was a relatively minor theological question. Duncan, who was not an ordained minister and therefore not allowed to administer the rite of communion, decided to forbid the practice at Metlakatla.

According to Duncan, his heathen charges might confuse the Christian practice with a ritual cannibalism long practiced in traditional Tsimshian spiritualism. When church officials balked, Duncan, after 25 years on the British Columbia coast, refused to compromise. Instead, he led over 800 of his followers to "New Metlakatla." Here, just a few miles up the coast on Annette Island near Ketchican in Alaska, Duncan was out of the reach of his Anglican sponsors. Although Duncan's new community never rose to the prominence it once enjoyed on the British Columbia coast, New Metlakatla continued to flourish during Duncan's lifetime. A small settlement, now just called Metlakatla, exists there today.

Commander John Pike Brings Devastation to Indians
Inside Passage, Venn Passage, Pike Island

Pike Island is named for Commander John Pike of the Royal Navy who, in the paddle sloop *Devastation,* policed these waters against whiskey traders between 1860 and 1864. Whiskey trading to Indians, who often seemed to be on the verge of rebellion along the coast, was illegal. As a result, it was a constant problem for colonial officials to uphold the law and keep the native population peaceful. For the most part, the north coast of what became British Columbia was simply too far from Victoria to police adequately, or for that matter, to be of much concern to colonial officials.

During his years on the coast, Commander Pike did capture several vessels attempting to trade liquor to the natives of the region. Pike is probably remembered most, however, for his retaliation against Indians at Clayoquot Sound after they captured and burned a whiskey trading vessel called the *Kingfisher,* killing the captain and crew in the process. Whiskey trading might have been reprehensible, but for colonial officials the killing of a white man by an Indian, no matter what the reason, was intolerable anywhere on British Columbia's coast.

Pike was sent to the area in the *Devastation,* along with the Royal Navy's *Sutlej,* and attacked the band of local Indians deemed responsible for the murders. Pike's mission was to punish the Indians and exact as much retribution as possible so as to impress upon them the costs of killing a white. Much of the Indian village was destroyed, and a large number of Indians were killed. Several others were taken prisoner and sent to Victoria. Afterward, Pike retired from the navy and returned to England.

Surveyor Tricked about Name
Inside Passage, Venn Passage, Clianchi Island

Clianchi Island's name is the result of a quiet prank played on the surveyor who mapped the islands in Venn Passage. The government hired a Tsimshian Indian from Metlakatla by the name of Herbert Clifton to be the surveyor's assistant during the field work. While surveying the then unnamed Clianchi Island, the surveyor excused himself to retreat to the forest to empty his bowels in the privacy of the wilderness. He was gone for what seemed an inordinate amount of time, leaving Clifton to wait alone. When the surveyor finally returned the two started work again without speaking. Suddenly, the government surveyor turned to Clifton and asked him the Indian name for the island. The surveyor said he wanted to use it for his map. Without hesitation, Clifton smiled and said Clianchi Island, which in Tsimshian means "defecated upon island." The surveyor never bothered to ask for the word's translation so, to this day, Clianchi Island remains the official name.

British Columbia's First Gold Rush Trades Three Lost Ships for Little Gold
Queen Charlotte Islands, Mitchell Harbour

The first large-scale immigration to what we know today as British Columbia came with the Fraser River and Cariboo gold rushes of the late 1850s and early 1860s. The province's first gold rush, however, brought few settlers and very little gold. It happened in the Queen Charlotte Islands in 1851 when a Haida Indian showed up at Fort Victoria with a 27-ounce (766-g) nugget. Native people on the coast knew about the white man's obses-

Haida Indians at Massett, 1800s.

sion with the yellow metal, and the Indian wanted 1,500 Hudson's Bay Company blankets in exchange for his large nugget. No record confirms that the trade was made, but the gold certainly sparked interest in the Queen Charlottes.

These islands had been discovered by Perez in 1774. They were named in 1787 by Captain George Dixon of the King George's Sound Company after his ship, the *Queen Charlotte*. As late as 1851, the islands were still unexplored along an ill-defined border with Russian Alaska. While the islands were, according to European law, a British possession, they were not officially part of the colony of Vancouver Island. They were, however, still in what the Hudson's Bay Company considered its territory. The company sent the *Una*, commanded by Captain Willie Mitchell (for whom today's harbor is named), north to look for gold after the nugget appeared in Victoria.

To an extent, Mitchell found what he wanted. The crew of the *Una* found a vein of gold 6" (15 cm) wide running parallel to the shore for 80' (24 m) along Mitchell Harbour. But mining the gold did not go well. Every time the men blasted some of the gold free, the watching Indians would madly scramble to recover the gold before the whites. Members of the crew, hurrying after the gold, often found themselves being tackled by Indians. Finally, with about $1,500 worth of gold on board—and reckoning that the Indians had at least as much—*Una* crew members decided to give up the project.

Bad luck was not left behind with the abandonment of the mine, however. On the way back to Victoria, the *Una* was wrecked in a storm off Neah Bay and the gold was lost. Having no other ship available for hunting gold in the Queen Charlottes, the Hudson's Bay Company gave up on the project entirely. By this time, though, the Americans also had heard of the Haida gold finds, and the first American vessel, the *Georgina,* sailed to the Queen Charlottes. But instead of landing miners, it promptly ran aground on the east coast of the islands. To complicate matters, the sailors were captured by the Haida, who by then had had enough gold mining on their land. A second American crew reached Mitchell Harbour, but returned to Olympia for trade goods when they heard of the fate of the *Georgina.* On their return, officers were able to exchange blankets and other trading goods for their countrymen. The *Georgina* had already been ransacked and burned.

About 10 other American ships also reached the Queen Charlottes in the following weeks. Almost all were stopped from mining by the Indians, who not surprisingly considered everything in the Charlottes theirs. At least one vessel, the schooner *Susan Sturgis,* was hijacked by the Haida. Members of the crew were released only when Hudson's Bay Company traders from Fort Simpson, near today's Prince Rupert, agreed to pay a ransom for their freedom. Again, the Indians stripped the vessel of what they wanted and destroyed the rest.

By 1853, when British officials finally made the Queen Charlottes part of Governor Douglas's official colonial responsibilities, the gold rush had passed. It had yielded only a few hundred dollars in gold, and it cost three sailing ships as well as the lives of several sailors.

Indians Used Iron Tools Before Columbus
West Coast, Queen Charlotte Islands

The use of iron tools has often been cited as one of the supposed benefits that came to Indian people with the arrival of Europeans in the Americas. In fact, however, native people on the British Columbia coast were already using iron tools before

Kwuna, Queen Charlotte Islands.

whites arrived. When Spanish commander Perez made the first white contact with British Columbia Indians in 1774, he noted that Haida women wore iron rings and bracelets. Perez's men also saw at least one iron harpoon head as well as several knife blades. Various iron tools of non-European origin have since been found along the coast as far south as Washington State.

The usual explanation for the discovery of these tools has been that, long before Columbus, a loose trading chain connected native people on the northwest Pacific coast with Asia. The link was undoubtedly via Alaskan coastal tribes, the Inuit and Asian hunters across the Bering Strait. There's even a Haida legend that claims the waters to the west of the Queen Charlottes were the tribe's source of iron.

It is also suspected that some accidental contact was made between British Columbia Indians and the Japanese before the arrival of Europeans. Presumably, the occasional Japanese fishing boat would be swept in storms from the familiar waters near Japan and washed ashore in North America. Several such stories are mentioned in recorded history. In 1831, for instance, two Japanese survivors of one such accident came ashore on the west coast of the Queen Charlottes. Here, they were taken prisoner and enslaved by the Haida. Two years later, Hudson's Bay traders at Fort Simpson heard of the men and bought their freedom from the Haida. Eventually, the fishermen returned to

Japan via London. Other Japanese junks washed ashore on Cape Flattery in Washington State and at Nootka Sound on Vancouver Island later in the 1800s.

One persistent story of Asian contact with British Columbia Indians begins on the western side of the Pacific. Ancient Chinese documents include a tale about the missionary monk Huei-Shin, who traveled extensively to the northeast of Imperial China in the fifth century. Huei-Shin returned to China in 499 after spending a number of years in a place he called Fusang. The people of Fusang, according to Huei-Shin's tale, were a coastal population with a highly evolved culture, although they did not have iron. Huei-Shin also reported that the people of Fusang had a written language and followed the Buddhist religion. Despite this discrepancy, some people have suggested that the monk's travels were embellished tales of a visit to the people of the Pacific coast of North America. At least two ceremonial figures resembling Buddha and reportedly dating from Huei-Shin's time have been unearthed at British Columbia archaeological sites, lending tenuous credence to the tale.

Directory of Coastal British Columbia Museums

Alberni Valley Museum
Echo Centre
4255 Wallace Street
Port Alberni BC v9y 3y6
(250) 723-2181

Alert Bay Museum
199 Fir Street
Alert Bay BC von 1ao
(250) 974-5420

Bowen Island Archives & Museum
1013 Senior Road
Bowen Island BC von 1go
(604) 947-2655

B.C. Aviation Museum
Pat Bay Airport
3-3539 Norseman
Sidney BC v8l 4r1
(250) 655-3300

B.C. Forest Museum
R.R. #4 Trans Canada Highway
Duncan BC v9l 3w8
(250) 746-1251

B.C. Golf Museum
2545 Blanca Street

Vancouver BC v6r 4n1
(604) 222-4653

B.C. Sugar Museum
123 Rogers Street
Vancouver BC v6b 3v2
(604) 253-1131

Campbell River Museum
470 Island Highway
Campbell River BC v9w 2b7
(250) 287-3103

CFB Esquimalt Naval & Military
Museum
Box 700, Station Forces
Victoria BC v9a 7n2
(250) 363-5655

Chamainus Valley Historical
Museum
9799 Water Wheel Crescent
Chemainus BC vor 1ko
(250) 246-2445

Cortes Island Museum
Beasley Road
Mansons Landing BC vop 1ko
(250) 935-6391

Courtenay & District Museum
360 Cliffe Avenue
Courtenay BC V9N 2H9
(250) 334-3611

Cowichan Valley Museum
Duncan Train Station
Canada Avenue
Duncan BC V9L 1T5
(250) 746-6612

Craig Heritage Park Museum
1243 E. Island Highway
Parksville BC V9P 2H4
(250) 248-6966

Cumberland Museum
2680 Dunsmuir Avenue
Cumberland BC V0R 1S0
(250) 336-2445

Delta Museum
4858 Delta Street
Delta BC V4K 2T8
(604) 946-9322

Denman Island Museum
111 Northwest Road
Denman Island BC V0R 1T0
(250) 335-0880

Elphinstone Pioneer Museum
716 Winn Road
Gibsons BC V0N 1V0
(604) 886-8232

Fort Rodd Hill & Fisgard Lighthouse National Historic Site
603 Fort Rodd Hill Road
Victoria BC V9C 2W8
(250) 478-5849

Gabriola Museum & Art Gallery
505 South Road

Gabriola Island BC V0R 1X0
(250) 247-9252

Haida Gwaii Museum at Qay'llna-
gaay
Second Beach Road
Skidegate BC V0T 1S0
(250) 559-4643

Heritage Park
Terrace Regional Museum Society
Kalum Street, Box 246
Terrace BC V8G 4A6
(250) 635-2508

Japanese Canadian National
Museum
571 East Broadway
Vancouver BC V5T 1X4
(604) 874-8090

Kaatza Station Museum
125 South Shore Road
Lake Cowichan BC V0R 2G0
(250) 749-6142

Kitimat Centennial Museum
293 City Centre
Kitimat BC V8C 1T6
(250) 632-7022
web site: http://www.sno.net/kit-
muse/

Langley Centennial Museum
9135 King Street
Fort Langley BC V1M 2S2
(604) 888-3922

Maritime Museum of BC
28 Bastion Square
Victoria BC V8W 1H9
(250) 385-4222

Museum of Northern BC
P.O. Box 669
Prince Rupert BC v8j 3s1
(250) 624-3207

New Westminster Museum
302 Royal Avenue
New Westminster BC v3l 1h7
(604) 521-7656

North Pacific Cannery Village
Museum
1889 Skeena Drive
Port Edward BC v0v 1g0
(250) 628-3538

North Vancouver Museum
209 West 4th Street
North Vancouver BC v7m 1h8
(604) 987-5618
web site:
http://www.district.north-
van.bc.ca/mvma/index.htm/

Port Clements Museum
45 Bayview Drive
Port Clements BC v0t 1r0
(250) 557-4484

Port Hardy Museum
Box 2126
Port Hardy BC v0n 2p0
(250) 949-8143

Port Moody Station Museum
2734 Murray Street
Port Moody BC v3h 1x2
(604) 939-1648

Powell River Historical Museum
4800 Marine Drive
Powell River BC v8a 4z5
(604) 485-2222

Royal British Columbia Museum
675 Belleville Street
Victoria BC v8w 9w2
(250) 387-2944

Saanich Pioneer's Society Museum
7910 E. Saanich Road
Saanichton BC v8m 1t4
(250) 656-5714

Saanich Historical Artifacts Society Museum
7321 Lochside Drive
Saanichton BC v0s 1m0
(250) 652-5522

Sidney Museum
9801 Seaport Place
Sidney BC v8l 4x3
(250) 656-1322

Sointula Museum
Sointula BC v0n 3e0
(250) 642-6351

Sooke Regional Museum
2070 Phillips Road
Sooke BC v0s 1n0
(250) 642-6351

Sunshine Coast Maritime
Museum
Mollys Lane
Gibsons BC v0n 1v0
(604) 886-4114

Surrey Museum
6022 176th Street
Surrey BC v3s 4e8
(604) 543-3456

U'Mista Cultural Centre
Front Street
Alert Bay BC v0n 1a0

(250) 974-5403
web site:
http://swiftly.com/umista/

University of BC Anthropology
Museum
6393 N.W. Marine Drive
Vancouver BC V6T 1Z2
(604) 822-6788

West Vancouver Museum
680 17th Street
West Vancouver BC V7V 3T2
(604) 925-7295

White Rock Museum
14970 Marine Drive
White Rock BC V4B 1C4
(604) 541-2221

Name Index